Family Circle | chicken and turkey cookbook

Family Circle

TURKEY and CHICKEN

COOKBOOK

A Practical Guide to creative cooking containing special material from Family Circle
Magazine and the Family Circle Illustrated Library of Cooking

ROCKVILLE HOUSE PUBLISHERS
GARDEN CITY, NEW YORK 11530

on the cover:
A dieter's choice, **Exotic Tandoori Chicken** is steeped in a spiced lemon yogurt marinade, then roasted.

on the back cover:
For a variation on the familiar poultry dinner, try Cornish hens in **Springtime Party Platter** (bottom) or **California Chicken** cooked in a crockery pot.

opposite title page:
A wok means Chinese and **Chinese Wok Chicken** is one dish that is sure to please.

Publishing Staff

Editor: MALCOLM E. ROBINSON
Design and Layout: MARGOT L. WOLF
Production Editor: DONALD D. WOLF

For Family Circle

Editorial Director: ARTHUR M. HETTICH
Editor Family Circle Books: MARIE T. WALSH
Assistant Editor: CERI E. HADDA

A QUICK METRIC TABLE FOR COOKS

Liquid Measures

1 liter	4¼ cups (1 quart + ¼ cup or 34 fluid ounces)	1 gallon	3.785 liters
1 demiliter (½ liter)	2⅛ cups (1 pint + ⅛ cups or 17 fluid ounces)	1 quart	0.946 liter
1 deciliter (1/10 liter)	A scant ½ cup or 3.4 fluid ounces	1 pint	0.473 liter
1 centiliter (1/100 liter)	Approximately 2 teaspoons or .34 fluid ounce	1 cup	0.237 liter or 237 milliliters
1 milliliter (1/1000 liter)	Approximately 1/5 teaspoon or .034 fluid ounce	1 tbsp.	Approximately 1.5 centiliters or 15 milliliters

Weights

1 kilogram	2.205 pounds	1 pound	0.454 kilogram or 453.6 grams
500 grams	1.103 pounds or about 17.5 ounces	½ pound	0.226 kilogram or 226.8 grams
100 grams	3.5 ounces	¼ pound	0.113 kilogram or 113.4 grams
10 grams	.35 ounce	1 ounce	28.35 grams
1 gram	0.035 ounce		

Linear Measures

1 meter	1.09 yards or 3.28 feet or 39.37 inches	1 yard	0.914 meter
1 decimeter (1/10 meter)	3.93 inches	1 foot	0.3048 meter or 3.048 decimeters or 30.48 centimeters
1 centimeter (1/100 meter)	0.39 inch	1 inch	2.54 centimeters or 25.4 millimeters
1 millimeter (1/1000 meter)	0.039 inch		

Contents

"Finger lickin' good," is a truly American way of preparing chicken, and **Marie Walsh's Fried Chicken** lives up to its name.

Introduction

Poultry is one of the most versatile meats available. Chicken and turkey come instantly to mind. But there are also Cornish hen, duck, and goose, to name a few others. And as there are so many different birds, so are there different ways to fix them—roasting, braising, stewing, oven frying and grilling, and, the most recent cooking method, crockery cooking.

As the birds are available year-round, you don't have to wait for a favorite season. Poultry is always available fresh or frozen in your market. Goose and duck may pose a problem, but most markets have them frozen during holiday or festival times.

And best of all, whichever bird you select to grace your table, you'll find it completely clean and ready to cook.

How you cook your bird depends upon its age and type. Cook tender, young birds any suitable method; more mature birds take longer cooking. Braise or stew them or reserve them for your crockery pot. Identify the age of the bird by the name on the label—broiler-fryers or roasters are younger birds; hens or stewing chickens, or yearlings indicate mature birds.

But whatever the age of the bird and whichever cooking method you use, you'll find a host of ready-to-use recipes in your **Chicken and Turkey Cookbook.**

Chicken For All Seasons

A century before Huey Long promised the people of Louisiana a ''chicken in every pot'' King Henry IV of France promised the same to his subjects. Before and since there have been many different ways to cook and prepare chickens. On the following pages are many intriguing ways you can prepare this bird.

HEARTY CHICKEN DISHES

Marie Walsh's Fried Chicken

There's plenty of excitement packed into this basket of fried chicken

Makes 4 servings.

1 broiler-fryer, cut up (about 2½ pounds)
3 cups water
1 tablespoon salt
2 teaspoons fines herbes
2 teaspoons onion sauté
2 teaspoons seasoned salt
2 envelopes or teaspoons instant chicken broth
¼ teaspoon seasoned pepper
1 cup all-purpose flour
  Fat for frying
  CHICKEN BROTH (recipe follows)
  CHICKEN GRAVY (recipe follows)

1 Cover chicken with a mixture of water and salt in a medium-size bowl. Chill at least 1 hour.
2 Whirl fines herbes, onion sauté, seasoned salt, instant chicken broth, and seasoned pepper in an electric blender or grind in a mortar and pestle until a very fine powder. Combine with flour in a plastic bag.
3 Remove chicken pieces, a few at a time, from water; shake in flour mixture while still wet, until thickly coated with flour.
4 Melt enough shortening or pour in enough vegetable oil to make a 1-inch depth in a large skillet or an electric deepfat fryer; heat to 375° on a deep-fry thermometer or until a cube of bread turns golden in 60 seconds.
5 Fry chicken pieces, turning once, 5 minutes

on each side. Lift out with a slotted spoon; drain well on paper towels.
6 When all pieces are fried; drain the fat from skillet. Add 1 cup CHICKEN BROTH to skillet; return chicken pieces; cover skillet.
7 Cook 25 minutes, or until chicken pieces are fork tender. Place on hot serving platter and keep warm in oven while making CHICKEN GRAVY.

CHICKEN BROTH—Makes about 3 cups. Place salted water in which chickens soaked, with chicken giblets in a small saucepan; add 2 onion slices and a handful of celery leaves. Cover and simmer 30 minutes.

CHICKEN GRAVY—Makes about 2½ cups. Strain and add remaining chicken broth to skillet; bring to boiling, stirring and scraping baked-on juices from bottom and side of pan. Make a smooth paste with ¼ cup all-purpose flour and ½ cup cold water in a small cup. Stir into boiling liquid; continue stirring and boiling for 1 minute. Season to taste with salt and pepper; darken with a little gravy coloring, if you wish. Add chopped giblets and simmer 2 minutes longer.

Double-Treat Roast Chicken

Let your guests choose their favorite dressing and share the delicious gravy

Roast at 375° for 1¼ hours.
Makes 8 servings

2 broiler-fryers (about 2½ pounds each)
3 cups water
  Handful of celery leaves
2 onion slices
½ teaspoon salt
  Dash of pepper
FRUITED GIBLET DRESSING (recipe follows)
JARDINIERE DRESSING (recipe follows)
4 tablespoons (½ stick) butter or margarine, melted
2 teaspoons aromatic bitters
  Chicken Gravy (recipe follows)

1 Remove chicken giblets from chickens and return chicken and livers to refrigerator. Combine giblets, water, celery leaves, onion slices, salt and pepper in medium-size saucepan. Heat

(continued)

to boiling; reduce heat and simmer 50 minutes. Add chicken livers and cook 10 minutes longer, or until giblets are tender. Trim and finely chop giblets. Strain and reserve broth.

2 Stuff one chicken with *Fruited Giblet Dressing* and one chicken with *Jardiniere Dressing.* Place in shallow roasting pan. Brush chickens with part of melted butter or margarine.

3 Roast in moderate oven (375°) basting several times with pan drippings, 1 hour. Stir bitters into remaining butter or margarine. Brush over chickens. Roast 15 minutes longer, or until chickens are golden. Place on heated serving platter and keep warm while making CHICKEN GRAVY. Garnish platter with bundles of cooked carrots and green beans and parsley, if you wish.

Fruited Giblet Dressing

Makes 1½ cups or enough to stuff one 2½-pound chicken

    1 large apple, pared, cored and chopped
    2 tablespoons butter or margarine
      Chopped giblets
 1½ cup soft bread crumbs (3 slices)
    3 tablespoons giblet broth
    ½ teaspoon salt
    ¼ teaspoon ground allspice
      Dash of pepper

Sauté apple until soft in butter or margarine in skillet. Stir in chopped giblets and cook 2 minutes. Stir in bread crumbs, broth, salt, allspice and pepper until well-blended.

Jardiniere Dressing

Makes 1½ cups or enough to stuff one 2½-pound chicken

    1 medium-size onion, chopped (½ cup)
    ½ cup finely chopped celery
    ½ cup finely chopped carrots
    2 tablespoons butter or margarine
    1 cup soft bread crumbs (2 slices)
    ½ teaspoon leaf savory, crumbled
    ½ teaspoon salt
      Dash of pepper

Sauté onion, celery and carrots until soft in butter or margarine in skillet. Stir in bread crumbs, savory, salt and pepper until well-blended.

Chicken Gravy

This is a simple yet perfect way to make gravy for chicken

Makes about 2½ cups

Stir 4 tablespoons flour into pan drippings. Cook, stirring constantly, 3 minutes. Blend in remaining giblet broth. (You should have 2½ cups.) Cook, stirring constantly, until mixture thickens and bubbles 3 minutes.

Little Chicken Roasts

Everyone rates a half chicken with the best pineapple stuffing! And a mild sweet-sour sauce goes with it

Roast at 375° for 1½ hours.
Makes 6 servings

    1 can (8¼ ounces) crushed pineapple
    3 cups soft bread crumbs (6 slices)
    ½ cup flaked coconut (from a 3½-ounce can)
    ½ cup chopped celery
    ½ teaspoon salt
    ¼ teaspoon poultry seasoning
    2 tablespoons bottled steak sauce
      Sweet-and-Sour Sauce (recipe follows)

1 Rinse chicken inside and out with cold water; drain, then pat dry. Sprinkle inside with salt.

2 Melt butter or margarine in a small saucepan. Drain syrup from pineapple into a cup and set aside for making glaze in Step 6.

3 Combine pineapple with bread crumbs, coconut, and celery in a medium-size bowl; drizzle 4 tablespoons of the melted butter or margarine over; toss with a fork until crumbs are lightly coated. (Save remaining butter or margarine for Step 5.)

4 Stuff neck and body cavities of chickens lightly with pineapple-bread mixture. Smooth neck skin over stuffing and skewer to back; tie legs to tail with heavy white string. Place chickens in a roasting pan.

5 Stir salt and poultry seasoning into saved 4 tablespoons melted butter or margarine in saucepan; brush part over chickens.

6 Roast in moderate oven (375°), basting several times with butter mixture, 1 hour. Stir saved pineapple syrup and steak sauce into any remaining butter in saucepan; brush generously over chickens.

7 Continue roasting, basting once or twice

Small in size, **Little Chicken Roasts** are large in flavor.

more, 30 minutes longer, or until drumsticks move easily and meaty part of thigh feels soft.
8 Remove chickens to heated serving platter; keep warm while making *Sweet-and-Sour Sauce.*
9 When ready to serve, cut away strings from chickens. Garnish platter with water cress and preserved mixed fruits, if you wish. Pass sauce in a separate bowl to spoon over.

SWEET-AND-SOUR SAUCE—Blend 2 tablespoons cornstarch into drippings in roasting pan; stir in 1 cup water. Cook, stirring all the time, just until mixture thickens and boils 3 minutes. Stir in 2 tablespoons brown sugar and 1 tablespoon lemon juice. Strain into heated serving bowl. Makes about 1¼ cups.

Polynesian Chicken Platter

Mild curry-bacon sauce glazes the chickens to a sparkly gold. Rice stuffing has a double-nut seasoning

Bake at 350° for 2 hours.
Makes 6 to 8 servings

2 roasting chickens (about 4 pounds each)
    Hilo Stuffing (recipe follows)
3 tablespoons butter or margarine, melted
    HILO STUFFING (recipe follows)
    CURRY-FRUIT GLAZE (recipe follows)

1 Rinse chickens inside and out with cold water; drain, then pat dry. Stuff neck and body cavities lightly with *Hilo Stuffing.* Smooth neck skin over stuffing and skewer to back; tie legs to tails with string.
2 Place chickens on a rack in a roasting pan; brush with melted butter or margarine.
3 Roast in moderate oven (350°) 1 hour.
4 Spoon part of the *Curry-Fruit Glaze* over each to make a thick coating. Continue roasting, basting two or three times with remaining glaze, 1 hour, or until drumsticks move easily and chickens are glazed.
5 Remove to a heated serving platter; cut away strings and remove skewers.

Hilo Stuffing

Macadamia nuts and coconut give this rice stuffing a gourmet flair

Makes 4 cups, or enough to stuff 2 four-pound chickens

1 cup uncooked regular rice
4 tablespoons (½ stick) butter or margarine
1 medium-size onion, chopped (½ cup)
2 envelopes instant chicken broth
    OR: 2 chicken bouillon cubes
2½ cups water
½ cup chopped macadamia nuts (from a 6-ounce jar)
½ cup flaked coconut (from a 3½-ounce can)

1 Sauté rice in butter or margarine, stirring often, just until golden in a large saucepan.
2 Stir in onion, chicken broth or bouillon cubes, and water; heat to boiling, crushing cubes, if

(continued)

using, with a spoon; cover. Simmer 20 minutes,
or until rice is tender and liquid is absorbed.
3 Sprinkle with nuts and coconut; toss lightly
to mix.

Curry-Fruit Glaze

Canned strained apples-and-apricots mellow
the flavor of this exotic sauce

Makes 1½ cups, or enough to glaze 2 four-
pound chickens

4 slices bacon, diced
1 medium-size onion, chopped (½ cup)
2 tablespoons flour
1 tablespoon sugar
2 teaspoons curry powder
½ teaspoon salt
1 tablespoon bottled steak sauce
1 cup water
2 tablespoons lemon juice
1 jar (4 ounces) baby-pack strained apples-
and-apricots

1 Sauté bacon until crisp in a medium-size
saucepan; remove and drain on paper toweling.
2 Stir onion into drippings in saucepan; sauté
just until soft. Stir in flour, sugar, curry powder,
and salt; heat until bubbly.
3 Stir in remaining ingredients and bacon. Simmer, stirring several times, 15 minutes, or until
thick.

HOW TO STUFF AND TRUSS POULTRY

First rinse bird completely clean with cold running water inside and out. Pat dry. Rub the
cavity lightly with salt.

1 Spoon stuffing lightly into neck (do not pack,
for stuffing expands when cooking). Pull neck
skin over the opening and fasten to back with
a skewer or toothpick.

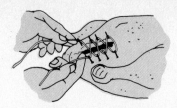

2 Stuff body cavity lightly. Close the opening
by running skewers or toothpicks through the
skin from one side of the opening to the other;
then lace securely with string in a crisscross
fashion. Or, you can sew the opening closed
with a large needle and thread.

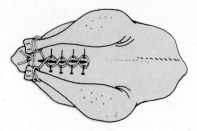

3 Loop the same string around the drumstick
ends and tie them together, then fasten them
to the tailpiece.

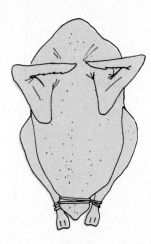

4 Fold wings up and over the back; this will
help brace the bird in the roasting pan. Brush
lightly with melted butter or margarine and
place, breast up, in a roasting pan.

Or, if barbecuing on a spit:

4 Press wings close to breast and run a string
around under the bird to completely encircle
it, securing the wings snugly against the breast.
The bird should be tied so that it makes a com-
pact bundle.

Country Roast Chicken

Wrap any leftovers immediately in foil or a plastic wrap and place in refrigerator for a second day feast

Bake at 350° for 1½ hours.
Makes 8 servings

2 broiler-fryers (about 3 pounds each)
1 cup water
½ teaspoon salt
1 package (8 ounces) corn bread stuffing mix
1 medium-size onion, chopped (½ cup)
½ cup sliced celery
½ cup (1 stick) butter or margarine
¼ cup bacon drippings
    OR: ¼ cup (½ stick) butter or margarine,
    melted

1 Remove giblets and necks from chicken packages and place (except livers) with water and salt in a small saucepan; cover. Simmer 45 minutes. Add livers; cover; simmer 15 minutes longer; cool.
2 Remove giblets and necks from broth; reserve broth. Chop giblets and the meat from necks; place in a large bowl; stir in stuffing mix.
3 Simmer reserved broth until reduced to ½ cup; reserve.
4 Sauté onion and celery in the ½ cup butter or margarine for 5 minutes in a medium-size skillet. Add with reserved broth to stuffing mixture in bowl; toss until evenly moistened.
5 Stuff neck and body cavities lightly with stuffing. Skewer neck skin to back; close body cavity and tie legs to tail. Place chickens on rack in roasting pan. Brush with part of bacon drippings or butter or margarine.
6 Roast in moderate oven (350°) basting every 30 minutes with bacon drippings or butter or margarine, 1½ hours, or until tender.
7 To serve: Place on heated serving platter. Cut chickens into quarters with poultry shears.

Monterey Chicken and Artichokes

Artichoke hearts and lemon rind add a California touch to chicken

Microwave for 13 minutes.
Makes 4 servings.

2 whole chicken breasts, boned (about 12 ounces each)
¼ cup milk
1 package (2⅜ ounces) seasoned coating for chicken
2 tablespoons butter or margarine, melted
1 package (8 ounces) frozen artichoke hearts
½ cup heavy cream
    Salt and pepper
    Grated rind of ½ lemon
3 slices bacon, cooked and crumbled

1 Cut chicken breasts in half; dip into milk in a pie plate, then in seasoned coating.
2 Melt butter or margarine in a 6-cup microwave-safe casserole in a microwave oven. Add chicken pieces, skin-side down.
3 Cook, uncovered, 3 minutes. Turn chicken pieces over. Add artichoke hearts, cream, salt and pepper. Cover with wax paper.
4 Cook 5 minutes. Turn dish. Add lemon rind; cover. Cook 5 minutes, or until chicken is tender. Top with crumbled bacon.

Parmigiana Chicken Cutlets

It's amazing how easily chicken cutlets can be substituted for veal in many classic veal cutlet dishes

Bake at 350° for 20 minutes.
Makes 4 individual casseroles.

8 chicken cutlets (about 1 pound)
1 egg
2 tablespoons water
1 teaspoon salt
¼ teaspoon seasoned pepper
½ cup Italian-seasoned fine dry bread crumbs
¼ cup olive oil or vegetable oil
1 jar (21 ounces) Italian cooking sauce
4 slices mozzarella cheese (from an 8-ounce package)

1 Place cutlets between pieces of wax paper and pound with a wooden mallet or rolling pin to flatten.
2 Beat egg with water, salt and seasoned pepper in a pie plate; place crumbs on wax paper. Dip cutlets, first into egg mixture, then into crumbs to coat lightly.
3 Brown cutlets, a few at a time, in hot oil in a large skillet. Drain on paper towels.
4 Spoon ¼ cup Italian cooking sauce into each of 4 individual casseroles; place two browned cutlets in each casserole; top with a slice of mozzarella cheese. Cover casseroles with plastic wrap and chill until meal time. Remove plastic wrap.

(continued)

5 Bake, one or two at a time, in preheated toaster-oven set to moderate (350°) 20 minutes, or until bubbly-hot.

Cook's Tip: To reheat in microwave oven, replace plastic wrap with wax paper; cook 5 minutes, turn casseroles, cook 5 minutes longer, or until bubbly-hot; let rest 2 minutes before serving.

ROASTING CHART FOR CHICKEN

Poultry	Ready-to Cook Weight	Oven Temp.	Guide to Roasting Time
Chicken	1½-2 lbs.	400°	1-1¼ hrs.
	2½-3 lbs.	375°	1¼-1½ hrs.
	3½-4 lbs.	375°	1¾-2 hrs.
	4½-5 lbs.	375°	2¼-2½ hrs.
Capon	4-7 lbs.	375°	2-3 hrs.

Tandoori Chicken

In India a chicken is marinated in yogurt and exotic herbs before roasting, for a dish that is delicious as well as low in calories

Roast at 350° for 1 hour, 30 minutes.
Makes 6 servings at 230 calories each.

1 roasting chicken (about 3½ pounds)
1 teaspoon saffron (optional)
1 tablespoon hot water
1 container (8 ounces) plain yogurt
¼ cup lime juice or lemon juice
2 cloves garlic, crushed
1½ teaspoons salt
1 teaspoon ground ginger
½ teaspoon ground cumin
½ teaspoon turmeric
   Dash cayenne pepper
   Watercress
   Lemon wedges

1 Skewer neck of chicken to body; push tail inside bird and secure body cavity closed; tie legs together and draw string up and under

wings and knot. Place in a large oval glass casserole.

2 Soak saffron in hot water for 5 minutes in a small bowl; stir in yogurt, lime or lemon juice, garlic, salt, ginger, cumin, turmeric, and cayenne. Spoon over chicken, coating evenly; cover casserole with plastic wrap. Marinate chicken for at least 4 hours, or overnight.

3 Roast in moderate oven (350°) 1 hour, 30 minutes, basting often with yogurt mixture, or until drumstick moves easily at joint; remove string.

4 Arrange on a heated serving platter with watercress and lemon wedges. Serve with a crisp salad of broken greens and sliced fresh mushrooms and cucumbers and a lemon-lime low-calorie drink, if you wish.

Romeo Salta's Chicken Scarpariello

"Scarpariello" in Italian means the shoe repair man: this might be a poor man's dish, but when you make it and taste it, you'll see it's fit for a king

Makes 6 to 8 servings.

2 broiler-fryers (2½ pounds each)
2 tablespoons olive oil
4 tablespoons butter
2 teaspoons salt
½ teaspoon freshly ground black pepper
1 clove garlic, minced
2 tablespoons chopped chives or green onions
¾ cup diced mushrooms
1½ cups dry white wine
½ cup chicken broth
½ pound chicken livers, cut in half
2 tablespoons minced parsley

1 To prepare recipe as Romeo Salta does: Have the chickens chopped up, bones and all, into small bite-size pieces, or use cut up chickens.

2 Heat the oil and 2 tablespoons butter in a large skillet; sauté the chicken in it until browned. Sprinkle with salt and pepper. Mix in the garlic and chives or green onions, then add the mushrooms, wine and broth.

3 Bring to boiling and cook over medium heat 30 minutes, or until chicken is tender.

4 Melt the remaining butter in a separate skillet; sauté the livers in it 5 minutes, or until very little pink remains. Season with a little salt and pepper. Add to the chicken; cook 5 minutes longer; top with parsley before serving.

HOW TO CARVE A CHICKEN

To carve roast chicken you need first of all a good, sharp, thin-bladed knife, and a sharp, long-tined fork. Keep your carving equipment in good condition, and do not use it for any purposes other than what it was intended for.

Before you begin to carve, be sure you remove from the chicken all the trussing equipment—skewers, toothpicks, cord, or thread.

Place the chicken breast side up on a serving platter or carving board large enough to make handling easy. You might have a separate plate nearby to hold drumsticks and wings out of the way as you remove them.

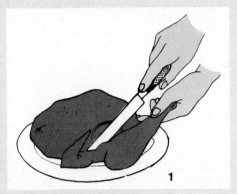

1 Place platter square in front of you, the chicken on its back with its legs toward your right. Grasping end of leg nearest you, bend it down toward platter while you cut through thigh joint to separate whole leg from body. Separate drumstick and thigh by cutting through joint.

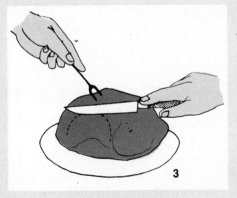

2 Stick fork into breast near breastbone and cut off wing close to body. Slanting knife inward slightly may make it easier to hit the joint.

3 Slice white meat, starting at tip of breastbone and cutting down toward wing joint. Repeat with other side of chicken, turning platter if you wish.

Chinese Wok Chicken

Stir-fry cooking is the answer to serving a fresh dish, when you're not sure when everyone will arrive

Makes 4 servings.

2 whole chicken breasts (about 12 ounces each)
⅓ cup soy sauce
⅓ cup sake, dry sherry or chicken broth
4 tablespoons peanut oil or vegetable oil
1 clove garlic, halved
1 small acorn squash, halved, seeded, cubed and cooked 5 minutes
1 cup cut green beans
1 small yellow squash, tipped and sliced
1 cup sliced mushrooms
1 package (6 ounces) frozen Chinese pea pods, thawed
1 package (10 ounces) fresh spinach, washed and trimmed
3 cups shredded Chinese cabbage

1 Remove skin from chicken and bone; cut into 1-inch pieces. Combine with soy and sake, sherry or chicken broth in a glass bowl; marinate.
2 Turn electric wok to 375° and add 2 tablespoons of the oil; heat until sizzling; add garlic and cook for 2 minutes; remove and discard garlic.
3 Remove chicken from marinade and drain on paper towels, reserving marinade. Cook chicken quickly in hot oil, stirring constantly; remove and keep warm.
4 Add remaining 2 tablespoons oil and heat; add acorn squash and green beans; toss until glistening with oil, push to one side; add yellow squash and mushrooms; toss in oil, then push to side; add pea pods, spinach and Chinese cabbage and toss until glistening.
5 Return chicken to wok with reserved marinade and toss to blend well; lower temperature to 200° and cover wok.
6 Simmer 5 minutes, or until vegetables are crisply-tender. Serve with boiled rice, if you wish.
Hostess Tip: All of the vegetables can be prepared ahead of time and arranged in a decorative pattern on a large flat tray; cover with plastic wrap and chill in refrigerator with marinating chicken. Cook at the table, when all the guests have arrived.

TYPES OF CHICKEN

Broiler-Fryer: Meaty, tender all-purpose chicken that can be cooked by any method. About 9 weeks old, broiler-fryers weigh 1½ to 3½ pounds.
Roaster: Slightly larger and older than broiler-fryers, roasters weight 3½ to 5 pounds and are best when roasted.
Stewing Chicken or Bro-Hen: A plump meaty bird, usually a year old or a little older that weighs 4½ to 6 pounds. These birds are tougher than broiler-fryers or roasters and are thus best when stewed or made into soup.
Capon: Fleshy, tender, desexed rooster with a high proportion of white meat and a fine flavor. Capons weigh 4 to 7 pounds and are excellent when roasted, steamed or stewed.
Chicken in Parts: In most markets today, it is possible to buy only that part of the chicken you want—all breasts, for example; or all drumsticks, all wings, thighs or backs.
Other Forms of Chicken: Besides the many kinds of fresh chicken available, you can also buy chicken frozen or canned—handy to have on hand as insurance against drop-in guests.

Classic Chicken Almond

An Oriental favorite of white meat, delicate vegetables and toasted nuts

Makes 6 servings.

3 whole chicken breasts, split (about 12 ounces each)
1 large onion, peeled and sliced
1½ teaspoons salt
⅛ teaspoon pepper
Water
2 tablespoons vegetable oil
1½ cups chopped celery
1 package (10 ounces), frozen peas
1 can (3 or 4 ounces) sliced mushrooms
2 tablespoons cornstarch
½ teaspoon ground ginger
¼ cup soy sauce
Toasted slivered almonds

1 Combine chicken breasts, 2 slices of the onion, salt, pepper and 1 cup water in a large saucepan; cover. Simmer 20 minutes, or until chicken is tender.

2 Remove from broth and cool until easy to handle; strain broth into a small bowl. Pull skin from chicken and take meat from bones in one piece; chill, then cut into thin strips. Chill broth separately, then skim fat, if needed.

3 When ready to finish cooking, sauté remaining onion in vegetable oil in a wok or large skillet 2 to 3 minutes; push to side. Stir in celery and sauté 2 to 3 minutes; push to side. Place peas, mushrooms and liquid and chicken strips in separate piles in pan; pour in broth; cover. Steam 10 minutes, or until peas are crisply tender.

4 Lift vegetables from pan with a slotted spoon; place in a serving bowl; lift out chicken strips and arrange on top of the vegetables. Keep warm while making sauce.

5 Blend cornstarch and ginger with soy sauce in a cup; stir in 2 tablespoons water until smooth. Stir into liquid in pan; cook, stirring constantly, until sauce thickens and bubbles 1 minute.

6 Spoon over chicken and vegetables; sprinkle with almonds. Garnish with thin strips of pimiento and serve with hot cooked rice or noodles, if you wish.

Hostess Tip: Chicken may be cooked as much as a day ahead and chilled in its broth to keep moist. Chop celery ahead too, and place in a plastic bag in the refrigerator until ready to cook.

Spanish Chicken Bake

New Spanish-rice-seasoning mix gives this dish a mellow slow-cooked flavor

Bake at 350° for 1 hour.
Makes 8 servings

2 broiler-fryers (about 2½ pounds each), quartered
¼ cup flour
¼ cup vegetable oil
1½ cups uncooked regular rice
3 cups water
1 envelope Spanish-rice-seasoning mix
1 large green pepper, cut in 8 rings
1 cup sliced stuffed green olives

1 Shake chicken with flour in paper bag to coat well. Brown, a few pieces at a time, in vegetable oil in large frying pan; drain on paper toweling.

(continued)

For a different taste-flavor try this happy combination of rice and chicken in **Spanish Chicken Bake.**

2 Place rice in a 10-cup shallow baking dish; arrange browned chicken on top.
3 Stir water into chicken drippings in frying pan; blend in Spanish-rice-seasoning mix; heat to boiling. Pour over chicken and rice; cover.
4 Bake in moderate oven (350°) 30 minutes; uncover and lay green-pepper rings and sliced olives on top. Cover and bake 30 minutes longer, or until chicken and rice are tender, and liquid is absorbed.

Japanese Chicken

Called Tori Sukiyaki, this one pot chicken and vegetable dish is prepared mostly at the table, each diner cooking his/her own in a simmering mixture of sugared soy sauce and sake (rice wine) or dry sherry

Makes 4 servings.

2 whole chicken breasts (about 12 ounces each)
1 bunch green onions
1 large onion
4 to 6 mushrooms
1 package (10 ounces) fresh spinach
  OR: 2 cups shredded Chinese cabbage
  OR: 1 bunch watercress
  OR: 1 cup sliced celery
1 package (4 ounces) thread noodles (harusame) (optional)
1 can (8 ounces) bamboo shoots (optional)
2 tablespoons peanut oil
½ cup soy sauce
2 tablespoons sugar
2 cakes soybean curd (tofu), cut into 1-inch cubes (optional)
½ cup mirin (sweet sake)
½ teaspoon monosodium glutamate

Prepare in advance:
1 Skin chicken breasts; cut meat from breast bones; slice into ⅛-inch-wide strips.
2 Trim green onions and cut into 3-inch pieces; cut onion into ½-inch slices and separate into rings; cut mushrooms into ¼-inch slices; wash and drain spinach well; remove stems and break into small pieces.
3 If harusame are available, bring 1 cup of water to a boil; drop in the harusame, return to the boil, then drain and cut noodles into thirds.
4 If bamboo shoots are available, pare and cut in half, lengthwise; cut into thin slices, crosswise, and wash under running water; drain.
5 Arrange chicken, vegetables and harusame

in neat rows on a large platter; cover platter with plastic wrap and refrigerate until serving time.
At the table for each serving:
6 Place a large skillet over a table burner and preheat for several minutes, or preheat an electric skillet to the highest setting (400° to 425°).
7 Rub part of oil over bottom of hot skillet.
8 Place one-fourth of the chicken in skillet; pour in 2 tablespoons of the soy sauce and sprinkle with part of the sugar. Cook for a minute, stirring and turning, then push to one side.
9 Add one-fourth of the vegetables (and tofu, harusame and bamboo shoots, if available); sprinkle with 2 tablespoons of the sake or dry sherry and monosodium glutamate. Cook, stirring often, 4 to 5 minutes longer, or until vegetables are crisply tender. (If food begins to stick or burn, lower heat and add a drop or two of cold water to the skillet.) Divide among 4 serving dishes; eat, then continue cooking and enjoying.

Casserole-Roasted Chicken

A one-dish meal for chicken lovers

Bake at 325° for 1¼ hours.
Makes 4 servings

1 broiler-fryer (about 3 pounds)
1½ teaspoon salt
¼ teaspoon pepper
16 small white onions, peeled
12 small red, new potatoes
3 tablespoons butter or margarine
3 tablespoons vegetable oil
½ cup boiling water
1 envelope instant chicken broth or 1 teaspoon granulated chicken bouillon
1 teaspoon leaf basil, crumbled
1 tablespoon chopped parsley

1 Sprinkle chicken cavities with ½ teaspoon of the salt and pepper. Peel onions. Scrub potatoes; pare a band around the center of each.
2 Melt butter or margarine with the vegetable oil in a large heavy flameproof casserole or Dutch oven. Add chicken; brown on all sides.
3 Combine boiling water and chicken broth in a 1-cup measure, stirring until dissolved; add to casserole with chicken.
4 Place onions and potatoes around chicken; sprinkle with basil and remaining 1 teaspoon salt; cover.

5 Bake in slow oven (325°), basting once or twice with juices, 1¼ hours, or until chicken and vegetables are tender. Sprinkle with parsley.

Chicken Imperial

Drumsticks, thighs, and breasts are stuffed with parsley-ham dressing, then breaded and baked in a creamy sauce

Bake at 350° for 1 hour and 15 minutes.
Makes 6 servings

2 cups soft bread crumbs (4 slices)
¾ cup finely diced cooked ham
½ cup chopped parsley
8 tablespoons (1 stick) hard butter or margarine, sliced thin
4 chicken breasts (about 12 ounces each)
4 chicken drumsticks with thighs
1 cup milk
1 cup fine dry bread crumbs
1 envelope (2 to a package) cream of mushroom soup mix
2 cups cold water
¼ cup chili sauce

1 Mix soft bread crumbs, ham, and parsley in a large bowl; cut in butter or margarine quickly with a pastry blender; chill while fixing chicken so butter doesn't melt.
2 Pull skin from chicken pieces; halve breasts, then cut out rib bones with scissors. Separate thighs and drumsticks at joints with a sharp knife. To make pockets for stuffing, pull each breast piece open on its thick side, and cut an opening along bone in each leg and thigh with a sharp-point knife.
3 Stuff about ¼ cup chilled stuffing into each half breast and 2 tablespoonfuls into each leg and thigh.
4 Place ½ cup of the milk in a pie plate and dry bread crumbs on a sheet of waxed paper. (Set remaining ½ cup milk aside for making sauce.) Roll stuffed chicken in milk, then in bread crumbs to coat well; chill while making sauce.
5 Combine mushroom soup mix and water in a small saucepan; cook, following label directions. Stir in remaining ½ cup milk and chili sauce; pour 1 cup into a shallow 12-cup baking dish.
6 Place chicken pieces, standing on edge if needed to fit, in sauce in dish; drizzle remaining sauce between pieces.

Chicken Imperial is the just-right dish when the company is special.

(continued)

7 Bake in moderate oven (350°) 1 hour and 15 minutes, or until tender and richly golden. Garnish with parsley, if you wish.
Hostess note—If dinner is delayed, simply lower oven heat to very slow (250°) and fit a sheet of foil, tent fashion, over casserole. It will hold well about an hour.

Baked Lemon Chicken

The flavors are subtle, but the result is a bird with a distinctive taste that you'll enjoy

Bake at 375° for 1 hour.
Makes 4 servings

1 broiler-fryer (about 2½ pounds)
½ cup flour
1¼ teaspoons salt
1 teaspoon leaf tarragon, crumbled
½ cup (1 stick) butter or margarine
⅓ cup lemon juice
1 tablespoon instant minced onion
1 clove of garlic, mashed
⅛ teaspoon pepper

1 Cut chicken into serving-size pieces.
2 Combine flour, 1 teaspoon of the salt, and tarragon in a plastic bag. Shake chicken in flour to coat; tap off excess.
3 Melt butter or margarine in a 13x9x2-inch baking pan. Coat chicken on all sides in melted butter or margarine, then turn pieces skin-side up.
4 Bake in moderate oven (375°), brushing often with pan drippings, 30 minutes.
5 Meanwhile, make Lemon Baste: Mix lemon juice, instant minced onion, garlic, remaining ¼ teaspoon salt, and pepper in a small bowl. Brush chicken pieces with part of the Lemon Baste.
6 Bake, brushing occasionally with remaining Lemon Baste, 30 minutes longer, or until chicken is tender.

Batter Crisp Chicken

Secret of this favorite is double cooking—baking first, then frying, covered with a puffy-golden jacket

Bake at 350° for 1 hour.
Makes 6 servings

2 broiler-fryers (about 2 pounds each), cut in serving-size pieces
2 teaspoons salt
1 teaspoon ground rosemary
½ cup water
Ginger Batter (recipe follows)
Shortening or vegetable oil for frying

1 Wash chicken pieces; pat dry. Place in a single layer in a large, shallow baking pan; sprinkle with salt and rosemary; add water; cover.
2 Bake in moderate oven (350°) 1 hour.
3 While chicken cooks, prepare GINGER BATTER.
4 Remove chicken from pan; pull off skin and remove small rib bones, if you wish; drain chicken well on paper toweling.
5 Melt enough shortening or pour in enough vegetable oil to make a 2-inch depth in an electric deep-fat fryer or large saucepan; heat to 350°.
6 Dip chicken pieces, 2 or 3 at a time, into *Ginger Batter;* hold over bowl to let excess drip back.
7 Fry in hot fat 3 minutes, or until golden-brown. Lift out with a slotted spoon; drain well. Keep hot until all pieces are cooked.

Ginger Batter

You bake the chicken first, then dip in this batter—and fry

Makes about 1½ cups

1¼ cups sifted all-purpose flour
1 teaspoon baking powder
1 teaspoon salt
½ teaspoon ground ginger
1 egg
1 cup milk
¼ cup vegetable oil

Sift flour, baking powder, salt, and ginger into a medium-size bowl. Add remaining ingredients all at once; beat with a rotary beater until smooth.

Oven-Barbecued Chicken

What a lazy-day way to turn out this picnic favorite! And it takes almost no watching

Bake at 400° for 1 hour.
Makes 4 servings

2 broiler-fryers (about 2 pounds each), quartered
1 large onion, cut into thick slices
⅔ cup catsup
⅓ cup vinegar
4 tablespoons (½ stick) butter or margarine
1 clove of garlic, minced
1 teaspoon leaf rosemary, crushed
1 teaspoon salt
¼ teaspoon dry mustard

Not every chicken with a barbecue glaze is turned over a spit on the coals. **Oven-Barbecued Chicken** didn't even see the outdoors.

1 Place chicken, skin-side down, in a single layer in a buttered shallow baking pan; top with onion slices.
2 Mix remaining ingredients in a small saucepan; heat to boiling; pour over chicken.
3 Bake in hot oven (400°) 30 minutes. Turn chicken, skin-side up; baste with sauce in pan. Continue baking, basting once or twice, 30 minutes longer, or until tender and richly glazed.

Old-Fashioned Chicken Pie

Keep in the goodness with a lattice crust

Bake at 400° for 30 minutes.
Makes 8 servings

2 *broiler-fryers (about 2½ pounds each)*
2 *cups water*
2 *teaspoons salt*
¼ *teaspoon pepper*
2 *cups sliced carrots*
1 *package (10 ounces) frozen peas*
¼ *cup (½ stick) butter or margarine*
6 *tablespoons flour*
1½ *cups biscuit mix*
½ *cup dairy sour cream*
1 *egg*
1 *tablespoon water*
2 *teaspoons sesame seeds*

1 Place chickens in a large heavy kettle or Dutch oven; add 2 cups water, salt, pepper, and carrots. Heat to boiling; reduce heat; cover; simmer 45 minutes. Add peas; simmer 15 minutes longer, or until chicken is tender. Remove chicken to a large bowl to cool.
2 Skim fat from chicken broth-vegetable mixture; reserve 2 tablespoons fat. Melt butter or margarine with reserved chicken fat in a medium-size saucepan; stir in flour; cook, stirring constantly, just until bubbly. Stir in chicken broth-vegetable mixture; continue cooking and stirring until gravy thickens and bubbles 1 minute.
3 When chickens are cool enough to handle, pull off skin and slip meat from bones; cut meat into bite-size pieces; stir into gravy; pour into an 8-cup baking dish, 8x8x2.
4 Combine biscuit mix and sour cream in a small bowl; stir to form a stiff dough; turn out onto a lightly floured board; knead a few times; roll out dough to ¼-inch thickness; trim to make an 8½-inch square; cut into 8 strips, each about one inch wide.
5 Using 4 of the strips, make a lattice design on top of the chicken mixture, spacing evenly and attaching ends firmly to edges of the dish. Place remaining strips, one at a time, on edges of dish, pinching dough to make a stand-up rim; flute rim. (Or, roll out dough to a 9-inch square and place over chicken mixture; turn edges under, flush with rim; flute to make a stand-up rim. Cut slits near center to let steam escape.)
6 Combine egg with 1 tablespoon water in a cup; mix with a fork until well-blended; brush mixture over strips and rim; sprinkle with sesame seeds.

7 Bake in hot oven (400°) 30 minutes, or until chicken mixture is bubbly-hot, and crust is golden. Serve immediately.

Chicken Stew

Big pieces of chicken bake in a zesty tomato sauce. Croutons add a pleasing crunch

Bake at 350° for 1 hour and 30 minutes.
Makes 8 servings

6 *slices bacon, cut in 1-inch pieces*
2 *broiler-fryers (about 2 pounds each), cut up*
½ *cup unsifted all-purpose flour*
2 *teaspoons salt*
¼ *teaspoon pepper*
1 *large onion, chopped (1 cup)*
1 *clove of garlic minced*
1 *can (3 or 4 ounces) whole mushrooms*
2 *cans (1 pound each) tomatoes*
¼ *cup chopped parsley*
Few drops liquid red pepper seasoning
Golden Croutons (recipe follows)

1 Fry bacon until almost crisp in large frying pan. Lift out with slotted spoon; drain on paper toweling and set aside for Step 6. Leave drippings in pan.
2 Wash and dry chicken pieces well. Snip off small rib bones with kitchen scissors, if you wish. Shake chicken in mixture of flour, salt, and pepper in paper bag to coat well. (Reserve any leftover flour mixture for Step 4.)
3 Brown chicken, a few pieces at a time, in bacon drippings; place in 12-cup shallow baking dish.
4 Saute onion and garlic until soft in same frying pan; stir in reserved flour mixture, drain liquid from mushrooms. (Save mushroom liquid for Step 6.) Stir liquid, tomatoes, parsley and red pepper seasoning into frying pan; heat to boiling, stirring constantly.
5 Spoon over chicken in baking dish; cover. (Casserole can be put together up to this point, then chilled. Remove from refrigerator and let stand at room temperature 30 minutes before baking.)
6 Bake in moderate oven (350°) 1 hour and 20 minutes, or until chicken is tender. Uncover; sprinkle with reserved bacon pieces and mushrooms. Bake 10 minutes longer, or until bacon is crisp.
7 Just before serving, sprinkle *Golden Croutons* over top; garnish with more chopped parsley, if you wish.

GOLDEN CROUTONS—Trim crusts from 2 slices white bread; cut into ½-inch cubes. Spread in single layer in shallow baking pan. Toast in moderate oven (350°) 10 minutes, or until golden. Makes 1 cup.

Chicken in Walnut Sauce

Take care with the directions, and the result will be stunning

Bake at 350° for 1¼ hours.
Makes 8 servings

1 package (8 ounces) regular noodles
2 broiler-fryers (about 2 pounds each), cut in serving-size pieces
2 teaspoons salt
½ teaspoon leaf rosemary, crumbled
¼ teaspoon pepper
3 tablespoons butter or margarine
1 medium-size onion, chopped (½ cup)
4 tablespoons flour
1¾ cups milk
¼ cup dry white wine
1 can (10¾ ounces) condensed cream of chicken soup
1 can (4 ounces) walnuts, chopped
Paprika

1 Cook noodles, following label directions; drain well. Place in a refrigerator-to-oven baking dish, 13x9x2.
2 Season chicken with 1½ teaspoons of the salt, rosemary, and pepper. Brown, part at a time, in butter or margarine in a large frying pan; place in a single layer over noodles.
3 Stir onion into drippings in pan; sauté until soft. Blend in flour; cook, stirring constantly, until bubbly. Stir in milk and wine; continue cooking and stirring until sauce thickens and boils 1 minute. Stir in soup, walnuts, and remaining ½ teaspoon salt. Pour over mixture in baking dish. Sprinkle with paprika. Cover; chill.
4 About 1 hour and 15 minutes before serving time, place baking dish, covered, in moderate oven (350°).
5 Bake 1 hour and 15 minutes, or until bubbly and chicken is tender.

Hong Kong Chicken

The quartered chicken lies in a bed of Chinese pea pods for an Oriental treat that's sure to please

Bake at 350° for 1½ hours.
Makes 4 servings

1 broiler-fryer (about 3 pounds)
¼ cup water
¼ cup dry sherry
¼ cup soy sauce
¼ cup honey
2 teaspoons seasoned salt

1 Cut chicken into quarters; arrange in a single layer in a 13x9x2-inch baking dish.
2 Mix water, sherry, soy sauce, honey, and seasoned salt in a small bowl; pour over chicken, turning to coat on all sides; cover. Marinate chicken in refrigerator about 4 hours, or overnight.
3 About 2 hours before serving time, remove chicken from refrigerator; let stand at room temperature 30 minutes, then drain; reserve marinade. Arrange chicken, skin side up, on rack in broiler pan, or in a shallow baking pan with a rack. Brush generously with part of the marinade.
4 Bake in moderate oven (350°), basting with remaining marinade every 20 minutes, 1½ hours, or until chicken is tender and deep golden brown. Place on heated serving platter; serve with cooked frozen Chinese pea pods and sliced water chestnuts, if you wish.

Golden Prize Party Chicken

Easiest way we know to cook chicken for a crowd

Bake at 350° for 1 hour.
Makes 8 servings, 2 pieces each

2 broiler-fryers (about 2-2½ pounds each), cut in serving-size pieces
½ cup evaporated milk
2 tablespoons prepared mustard
2 teaspoons salt
½ teaspoon marjoram
1 cup packaged corn-flake crumbs
¼ cup chopped parsley
1 green onion, chopped

(continued)

1 Cut away small bones from chicken breasts; remove all skin if you prefer chicken cooked without it. (Cook with backs and necks to make broth for another meal.)
2 Combine evaporated milk, prepared mustard, 1 teaspoon salt, and marjoram in pie plate; combine cornflake crumbs, parsley, green onion, and remaining 1 teaspoon salt in second pie plate.
3 Dip chicken pieces, 1 at a time, in evaporated-milk mixture; drain well, then roll in crumb mixture; arrange in single layer, pieces not touching, on cooky sheet lined with buttered aluminum foil.
4 Bake in moderate oven (350°) 1 hour, or until chicken is richly browned and tender when pierced with a fork.

"Coq Au Vin"

Long slow cooking gives this aristocrat the mellowest flavor. Its seasoning secrets: Apple cider and mixed vegetable juices

Bake at 350° for 2 hours and 15 minutes.
Makes 4 servings

1 stewing chicken (about 4 pounds), cut in serving-size pieces
⅓ cup unsifted all-purpose flour
1½ teaspoons salt
3 tablespoons butter or margarine
½ cup diced cooked ham
12 small white onions, peeled
1 can (12 ounces) mixed vegetable juices (1½ cups)
1½ cups apple cider
1 can (3 or 4 ounces) mushroom caps
1 clove garlic, minced
6 peppercorns
6 whole cloves
1 bay leaf

1 Wash chicken pieces; pat dry. Shake with flour and salt in a paper bag to coat well.
2 Brown pieces, a few at a time, in butter or margarine in a large frying pan; place in a 12-cup baking dish; sprinkle with ham and top with onions.
3 Stir vegetable juices, cider, mushrooms and liquid, and garlic into drippings in pan; heat to boiling, scraping brown bits from bottom of pan. Pour over chicken mixture.
4 Tie seasonings in a tiny cheesecloth bag; add to baking dish; cover.

5 Bake in moderate oven (350°) 2 hours and 15 minutes, or until chicken is very tender.
6 Uncover; remove spice bag and let chicken stand for 5 to 10 minutes, or until fat rises to top, then skim off. Garnish chicken with parsley, if you wish.

Chicken Sauté, Normandy Style

Apple cider is the secret ingredient that gives this dish the flavor of the Normandy region of France

Makes 6 servings

2 broiler-fryers (about 1½ pounds each)
1 tablespoon vegetable oil
2 tablespoons butter or margarine
2 tablespoons applejack
1 medium-size onion, finely chopped (½ cup)
½ cup sliced celery
2 tablespoons chopped parsley
1 teaspoon salt
¾ teaspoon leaf thyme, crumbled
⅛ teaspoon pepper
1 cup apple cider
2 egg yolks
1 cup light cream or table cream

1 Cut chickens into serving-size pieces. Brown well on all sides in oil and butter or margarine in a large heavy kettle or Dutch oven; remove from heat.
2 Warm the applejack in a small saucepan until small bubbles appear around edge. (Do not boil.) Carefully ignite with a wooden match held at arm's length. Quickly pour over chicken, shaking gently until flames die. Remove chicken to a heated platter; keep warm.
3 Sauté onion and celery until soft in same kettle. Stir in parsley, salt, thyme, pepper, and cider; heat to boiling. Return chicken pieces; reduce heat; cover. Simmer 45 minutes, or until chicken is tender; remove from heat. Remove chicken pieces from cooking liquid to a heated serving platter; keep hot.
4 Beat egg yolks slightly in a small bowl; blend in light cream. Gradually add cooking liquid, beating vigorously; pour back into saucepan. Cook, over medium heat, stirring constantly, 1 minute, or until sauce thickens slightly. Pour a little of the sauce over chicken pieces. Pass remaining sauce separately.

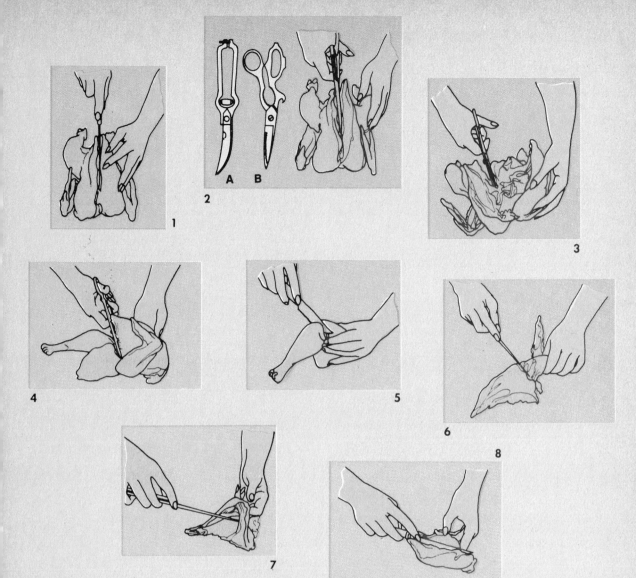

HOW TO CUT AND BONE A CHICKEN

1 Place chicken breast side up. Using a sharp knife, make lengthwise slit through skin and flesh from neck to cavity. Turn bird over and repeat cut.

2 Using poultry shears (**A**) or kitchen shears (**B**), cut right through bones (ribs). Cutting to one side of breastbone is easier than cutting through it.

3 Turn chicken over. Cut through bones, cutting to one side of the backbone. You may remove backbone. A small bird is cut this way for serving.

4 For quartering chicken, continue using shears. Cut across half the bird, following the natural division just below the rib cage and the breastbone.

5 Thigh may be left attached to leg for broiling; but for frying, bend leg joint. Cut through joint with a sharp knife, separating leg from the thigh.

6 To separate wing from the breast, bend joint. Cut through joint with a sharp knife. The chicken will now be in eight pieces and ready for frying.

7 If your recipe calls for skinned chicken breasts, use a sharp, small paring knife to start, then slip fingers between skin and flesh and peel skin.

8 To bone chicken breast, use a small paring knife. Cut meat away from rib bones with quick little strokes, feeling your way along with your fingers.

Chicken Paprikash

There is plenty of flavor and nutrition in this Hungarian favorite

Makes 8 servings

2 broiler-fryers (about 3 pounds each)
2 tablespoons butter or margarine
1 large onion, chopped (1 cup)
2 tablespoons paprika
1 tablespoon flour
3 teaspoons salt
¼ teaspoon pepper
1 can (8 ounces) tomatoes
1 cup (8-ounce carton) dairy sour cream
1 tablespoon chopped parsley
1 package (1 pound) noodles

1 Cut chickens into serving-size pieces.
2 Sauté onion in butter or margarine until soft in a large skillet with a cover. Stir in paprika and flour; cook, stirring constantly, 1 minute. Stir in salt, pepper, and tomatoes (breaking with spoon).
3 Add chicken and giblets (except livers), turning to coat pieces well; cover. Simmer 30 minutes. Turn chicken pieces; add livers; simmer 15 minutes longer, or until chicken is tender.
4 Meanwhile, cook noodles, following label directions; drain; spoon onto hot serving platter. Remove chicken from skillet with a slotted spoon. Arrange on platter with noodles; keep warm.
5 Spoon sour cream into a medium-size bowl. Heat sauce in skillet to boiling; stir slowly into sour cream, blending well. Spoon over chicken.

Chicken, Hunter's Style

You don't have to be in the fields to enjoy this dish

Makes 4 servings

1 broiler-fryer (about 3 pounds)
1 tablespoon vegetable oil
1 tablespoon butter or margarine
¼ pound mushrooms, trimmed and sliced
2 large tomatoes, peeled, seeded and chopped
¼ cup sliced green onions
1 small clove of garlic, crushed
¾ cup water
2 tablespoons lemon juice
1 teaspoon leaf chervil or thyme, crumbled
1 teaspoon salt

⅛ teaspoon pepper
1 teaspoon cornstarch

1 Cut chicken into serving-size pieces. Brown in oil and butter or margarine in a large skillet with a cover.
2 Add mushrooms, tomatoes, green onions, garlic, ½ cup of the water, lemon juice, chervil, salt, and pepper; cover. Simmer 45 minutes, or until chicken is tender. Remove chicken to a heated serving platter; keep hot.
3 Blend cornstarch with remaining water in a cup; stir into liquid in skillet. Cook, stirring constantly, until mixture thickens and bubbles 3 minutes. Pour over chicken; serve at once.

Chicken Cacciatore

Men often order this zesty Italian favorite when eating out. It's a good choice, too, for guests, for it waits perfectly

Makes 8 servings

2 broiler-fryers (about 3 pounds each), quartered
¾ cup unsifted all-purpose flour
3 teaspoons salt
¼ teaspoon pepper
6 tablespoons olive oil or vegetable oil
1 large onion, chopped
1 clove garlic, minced
1 can (about 2 pounds) Italian tomatoes
1 tablespoon sugar
1 teaspoon leaf basil, crumbled
½ teaspoon leaf thyme, crumbled
2 medium-size green peppers, halved, seeded, and sliced

1 Wash chicken quarters; pat dry. Shake with flour, salt, and pepper in a paper bag to coat well.
2 Brown pieces, a few at a time, in olive oil or vegetable oil in a large frying pan; remove all from pan.
3 Stir onion and garlic into drippings in pan and sauté until soft; stir in tomatoes, sugar, basil, and thyme; heat to boiling.
4 Return chicken to pan; spoon some of the tomato sauce over; lay sliced green peppers on top; cover.
5 Simmer, basting several times with sauce in pan, 1½ hours, or until chicken is tender.

Chicken Cacciatore is usually quartered. For a variation, cut up the chicken into bite-size pieces and serve with an unusual shaped pasta. Everyone will enjoy this new way with an old-time favorite.

Twin Chickens Parisiennes

Stuff each with a whole bunch of parsley and simmer in a savory mushroom sauce to serve with noodles

Makes 6 to 8 servings

2 broiler-fryers (about 3 pounds each)
1 teaspoon salt
½ teaspoon sugar
2 bunches parsley, washed and trimmed
2 tablespoons butter or margarine
1 can (3 or 4 ounces) whole mushrooms
¼ teaspoon pepper
2 tablespoons flour
¾ cup light or table cream
   Hot cooked noodles

1 Rinse chickens inside and out with cold water; drain, then pat dry. Sprinkle insides with ½ teaspoon of the salt and sugar; place parsley in body cavities, packing in lightly. Skewer neck skin to back; twist wing tips flat against skewered neck skin; tie the legs to tails with string.
2 Brown in butter or margarine in a heavy kettle or Dutch oven; turn breast side up.
3 Drain liquid from mushrooms into a 1-cup measure; add water to make ¾ cup; pour over chickens. Sprinkle with remaining ½ teaspoon salt and pepper; cover tightly. (Set mushrooms aside for Step 6.)
4 Simmer, basting several times with liquid in kettle, 1 hour and 15 minutes, or until tender. Remove from kettle and keep hot while making gravy.
5 Pour liquid from kettle into a 2-cup measure; let stand about a minute, or until fat rises to top, then skim off into a cup. Add water to liquid, if needed, to make 1 cup.
6 Measure 2 tablespoonfuls of the fat and return to kettle; blend in flour; stir in the 1 cup liquid.

(continued)

Cook, stirring constantly, until gravy thickens and boils 1 minute. Stir in mushrooms and cream; heat slowly just to boiling. Darken with a few drops bottled gravy coloring, if you wish.
7 Spoon noodles into a heated large serving bowl. Take out skewers and cut strings from chickens; arrange chickens on top of noodles; spoon gravy over all. Garnish with parsley, if you wish. Carve chickens into serving-size pieces.

Chicken Tetrazzini

For a new way with an old casserole favorite, try cooking it this way

Makes 6 servings

1 broiler-fryer (2½ to 3 pounds), cut up
1 small onion, peeled and sliced
  Few celery tops
1 teaspoon salt
  Water
1 can (3 or 4 ounces) sliced mushrooms, drained
1 cup thinly sliced celery
1 envelope old-fashioned French salad dressing mix
  Vegetable oil
  Cider vinegar
1 package (8 ounces) thin spaghetti, broken in 1-inch lengths
½ cup light cream or table cream
¾ cup mayonnaise or salad dressing
½ pound Swiss cheese, shredded
2 cups shredded iceberg lettuce

1 Combine chicken, onion, celery tops, salt, and 1 cup water in a medium-size frying pan; cover. Simmer 45 minutes, or until chicken is tender. Remove from broth; cool until easy to handle, then pull off skin and take meat from bones; dice meat. Strain broth and chill for soup another day.
2 Combine chicken with mushrooms and celery in a medium-size bowl.
3 Prepare salad dressing mix with vegetable oil, vinegar, and water, following label directions; drizzle ¼ cup over chicken mixture; toss lightly; chill.
4 Cook spaghetti, following label directions; drain well. While warm, combine with cream and ½ cup of the mayonnaise or salad dressing in a medium-size bowl; toss until evenly coated. Fold in cheese; chill.
5 When ready to serve, place lettuce in a large

shallow serving dish; spoon spaghetti mixture on top. Fold remaining ¼ cup mayonnaise or salad dressing into chicken mixture; mound in center of spaghetti. Sprinkle lightly with paprika, if you wish.

Curried Chicken

A spicy taste of India brings a surprise to this new chicken dish

Makes 4 servings

2 tablespoons curry powder
4 tablespoons (½ stick) butter or margarine
3 medium-size onions, chopped (1½ cups)
2 tablespoons flour
½ teaspoon ground ginger
2 chicken bouillon cubes
2 cups water
1 can (8¼ ounces) crushed pineapple
3 cups diced cooked chicken or turkey
2 tablespoons lemon juice
4 cups hot cooked rice

1 Heat curry powder in butter or margarine in large frying pan, stirring often, 2 to 3 minutes. Stir in onions and cook until softened.
2 Blend in flour and ginger, then add bouillon cubes, water, and pineapple and syrup. Heat to boiling, stirring until cubes are dissolved; simmer, uncovered, 5 minutes.
3 Stir in chicken; cover; simmer 10 minutes longer, or until heated through. Stir in lemon juice; serve over rice.

Chicken Parmigiana

Chicken goes well in this classic dish—all the family will enjoy this variation

Makes 6 servings

3 chicken breasts, (about 12 ounces each), split, skinned, and boned
2 eggs, lightly beaten
1 teaspoon salt
⅛ teaspoon pepper
¾ cup fine dry bread crumbs
½ cup vegetable oil
2 cans (8 ounces each) tomato sauce
¼ teaspoon basil

⅛ teaspoon garlic powder
1 tablespoon butter or margarine
½ cup grated Parmesan cheese
8 ounces mozzarella cheese, sliced and cut
into triangles

1 Place chicken breasts on cutting board and pound lightly with side of heavy knife or cleaver until about ¼ inch thick.
2 Combine eggs, salt, and pepper. Dip chicken into egg mixture, then crumbs.
3 Heat oil until very hot in a large frying pan. Quickly brown chicken on both sides; remove to shallow baking dish. Pour excess oil from frying pan.
4 Stir tomato sauce, basil, and garlic powder into frying pan; heat to boiling; simmer 10 minutes, or until thickened. Stir in butter or margarine. Pour over chicken; sprinkle with cheese; cover.
5 Bake in moderate oven (350°) 30 minutes; uncover.
6 Place mozzarella over chicken. Bake 10 minutes longer, or until cheese melts.

Stuffed Boneless Breasts of Chicken

When the company is special, look no further for a special recipe

Makes 4 servings

2 cups ready-mix bread stuffing
2 chicken breasts, (about 12 ounces each), split and boned
2 tablespoons butter or margarine, melted
½ teaspoon salt
¼ teaspoon pepper
¼ teaspoon garlic powder
¼ teaspoon paprika
1 can (10¾ ounces) condensed cream of mushroom soup
½ cup dry white wine

1 Make stuffing, following label directions.
2 Generously butter a baking dish, 8x8x2. Divide stuffing into 4 equal mounds in baking dish. Top each with a half chicken breast, tucking meat down around stuffing to cover completely. Brush with butter or margarine, sprinkle with salt, pepper, garlic powder, and paprika.
3 Bake in moderate oven (350°) 1 hour, or until golden.
4 Combine soup and wine in a small saucepan; heat slowly, stirring constantly, until bubbly. Pour over chicken and serve.

Chafing-Dish Chicken Royale

Perfect for a company buffet. Shrimps and tiny meat balls add the royal touches

Makes 6 servings

3 chicken breasts (about 12 ounces each), halved
4 cups water
Few celery tops
2½ teaspoons salt
½ pound meat-loaf mixture (ground beef and pork)
6 tablespoons flour
Dash of pepper
1 egg
2 teaspoons grated onion
¼ cup milk
3 medium-size carrots, pared and sliced
1 cup frozen peas (from a 1¼-pound bag)
4 tablespoons (½ stick) butter or margarine
1 tablespoon lemon juice
Few drops liquid red pepper seasoning
1 can (about 5 ounces) deveined shrimps, drained and rinsed
2 tablespoons chopped parsley

1 Combine chicken breasts, water, celery tops, and 2 teaspoons of the salt in a large saucepan; cover. Simmer 30 minutes, or until chicken is tender.
2 Remove from broth and cool until easy to handle. Pull off skin and take meat from bones in one piece; set aside for Step 7. Set broth aside for Step 4.
3 Combine meat-loaf mixture, 2 tablespoons of the flour, remaining ½ teaspoon salt, pepper, egg, onion, and milk in a medium-size bowl; mix with a fork until well-blended. Shape into 18 small balls. (Set remaining flour aside for making sauce.)
4 Reheat chicken broth to boiling; add meat balls; cover. Poach 10 minutes or until cooked through; lift out with a slotted spoon and place in a bowl.
5 Cook carrots, covered, in part of the same chicken broth 20 minutes, or until tender; cook peas in remaining broth, following label directions. Drain liquid from each and strain into a 4-cup measure; add more water, if needed, to make 4 cups. Keep carrots and peas hot for Step 7.
6 Melt butter or margarine in a large saucepan; blend in remaining 4 tablespoons flour; cook, stirring constantly, just until bubbly. Stir in the 4 cups chicken broth; continue cooking and

(continued)

stirring until sauce thickens and boils 1 minute. Stir in lemon juice and red pepper seasoning.
7 Cut each half chicken breast into three pieces; add to sauce with meat balls, carrots, and peas. Heat slowly just to boiling; spoon into a chafing dish or heated serving dish. Arrange shrimps on top; sprinkle with parsley.

Asparagus Chicken

The title may sound delicate, but there's plenty of fullness in this dish

Makes 6 servings

    3 chicken breasts (about 10 ounces each), skinned and boned
    6 tablespoons vegetable oil
    ½ pound asparagus
    1 bunch green onions, trimmed and sliced thin (¾ cup)
    1 can (3 or 4 ounces) sliced mushrooms
    1 can (10¾ ounces) condensed chicken broth
1½ teaspoons ground ginger
    1 teaspoon salt
    1 teaspoon sugar
    ¼ teaspoon garlic powder
    2 tablespoons cornstarch
    ⅓ cup dry sherry
    3 tablespoons soy sauce
    4 cups cooked rice

1 Slice chicken in thin strips about 1½ inches long.
2 Heat 4 tablespoons of the vegetable oil in a large frying pan. Stir in chicken; sauté, stirring several times, 4 minutes, or until chicken turns white. Remove from frying pan to a bowl; keep warm for Step 4.
3 Break tough woody ends from asparagus; wash stalks in cold water. If scales are large or sandy, cut off with a sharp knife, then wash stalks again; drain well. Split each stalk lengthwise, then cut in 1½-inch lengths.
4 Heat remaining 2 tablespoons vegetable oil in same frying pan. Stir in asparagus and onions; sauté 2 minutes. Stir in chicken, mushrooms and liquid, chicken broth, ginger, salt, sugar, and garlic powder; cover. Simmer 3 minutes.
5 Mix cornstarch, sherry, and soy sauce until smooth in a cup; stir into mixture in frying pan. Cook, stirring constantly, until mixture thickens and boils 3 minutes. Serve over rice.

HOW MUCH CHICKEN TO BUY

Here are rules to follow in deciding how much chicken to buy, although you may want to increase these portions for big eaters in the family:

Chicken for Frying: *Allow ¾ to 1 pound per serving.*
Chicken for Roasting: *Allow ¾ to 1 pound per serving.*
Chicken for Broiling or Barbecuing: *Allow ½ chicken or 1 pound per serving.*
Chicken for Stewing: *Allow ½ to 1 pound per serving.*

Count on about 1 cup of cut-up cooked meat from each 1 pound of uncooked stewing chicken. You will need more when making a salad, or slicing for sandwiches and cold cuts, than when fixing a casserole or creamed dish.

Mandarin Chicken Breasts

Save this dish for the night of the Chinese New Year

Makes 6 servings

    6 chicken breasts (about 12 ounces each), boned
      Salt
1½ cups hot cooked rice
    3 tablespoons butter or margarine
    1 tablespoon chopped parsley
    ¼ teaspoon leaf rosemary, crumbled
    ¼ teaspoon leaf basil, crumbled
    ¼ cup unsifted all-purpose flour
    ½ teaspoon paprika
    2 envelopes instant chicken broth or 2 teaspoons granulated chicken bouillon
1¾ cups water
    1 tablespoon instant minced onion
    2 tablespoons lemon juice
    1 bay leaf
    1 tablespoon cornstarch
    1 can (about 11 ounces) mandarin orange segments, drained
    1 cup seedless green grapes

1 Sprinkle insides of chicken breasts lightly with salt.
2 Combine rice, 1 tablespoon of the butter or

margarine, ¼ teaspoon salt, parsley, rosemary, and basil in a large bowl; toss lightly to mix; spoon into hollows in chicken breasts. Fold edges over stuffing to cover completely; fasten with wooden picks.

3 Mix flour, paprika, and ½ teaspoon salt in a pie plate; dip chicken breasts into mixture to coat well. Brown slowly in remaining 2 table-spoons butter or margarine in a large frying pan.

4 Stir in chicken broth, water, onion, lemon juice, and bay leaf; heat to boiling; cover.

5 Simmer 25 minutes, or until chicken is tender; remove bay leaf. Place chicken on a heated deep serving platter; keep warm. Reheat liquid to boiling.

6 Smooth cornstarch with a little water to a paste in a cup; stir into liquid in frying pan. Cook, stirring constantly, until sauce thickens and boils 3 minutes. Stir in mandarin orange segments and grapes; heat until bubbly. Spoon over chicken. Garnish with additional grapes and mandarin-orange segments threaded onto a long skewer.

Chicken Kiev

This spectacular, with its parsley-butter stuffing that spills out as you cut each roll, is fussy to make so prepare ahead

Makes 6 servings

1½ sticks (6 ounces) butter or margarine
6 chicken breasts (about 12 ounces each)
4 tablespoons finely chopped parsley
½ teaspoon sugar
2 eggs
1 cup fine dry bread crumbs
1 teaspoon salt
⅛ teaspoon pepper
Shortening or vegetable oil for frying

1 Cut butter or margarine into 12 even-length sticks; chill in freezer while fixing chicken, for butter should be *very* cold.

2 Pull skin from chicken breasts; halve breasts and cut meat in one piece from bones. Place each half, boned-side up, between wax paper and pound very thin with a mallet or rolling pin to form a "cutlet." (Be careful not to pound holes in meat.)

3 Place 1 piece very cold butter or margarine, 1 teaspoon parsley, and a dash of the sugar

on end of each cutlet; fold sides over to seal in butter, then roll up. Hold in place with wooden picks.

4 Beat eggs slightly in a pie plate; mix bread crumbs, salt, and pepper in a second pie plate. Dip stuffed rolls in egg, then in crumb mixture to coat well. Chill at least an hour. (This much can be done ahead.)

5 When ready to fry, melt enough shortening or pour in enough vegetable oil to make a 2-inch depth in an electric deep-fat fryer or large saucepan; heat to 350°.

6 Fry rolls, 3 to 4 at a time and turning often, 7 minutes, or until tender and crisply golden. Lift out with a slotted spoon; drain well. Keep hot until all rolls are cooked.

Just-Right Fried Chicken

This is the kind of fried chicken that will boost your fame handsomely high. Cook it slowly (it just can't be hurried) and it will come out with the crispest golden jacket hiding the tenderest sweet meat—every time.

Buy plump broiler-fryers weighing about 3 pounds each. Cut each into 8 serving-size pieces—2 breasts, 2 wings, 2 thighs, 2 drumsticks. Simmer bony back pieces to make broth for gravy, if you wish. To coat and season each chicken you'll need:

½ cup unsifted all-purpose flour
1 teaspoon salt
⅛ teaspoon pepper

And for frying:

1 cup bacon drippings or part drippings and shortening

1 Wash chicken, but do not dry. This is impor-tant so skin will take on a thick flour coating. Mix flour, salt, and pepper in a bag. Shake pieces, a few at a time, to coat evenly all over

2 Heat a quarter-inch depth bacon drippings in an electric skillet to 360°, or use a large heavy frying pan on medium heat. Arrange chicken, without crowding, in a single layer in hot fat

3 Brown slowly for 15 minutes. When pink juices start to show on top, turn and brown the other side 15 minutes. It's the slow cooking, plus *turning just once*, that gives chicken its crisp coating

4 When pieces are browned, pile all into skillet and cover. Reset control at 260°, or lower range heat to simmer. Let chicken cook 20 minutes longer, or until it's richly golden and fork-tender.

Country Fried Chicken

Nothing quite equals crispy-brown fried chicken in popularity—and here's how

Makes 6 to 8 servings

2 broiler-fryers (about 2 pounds each), cut into
  serving-size pieces
⅔ cup unsifted all-purpose flour
2 teaspoons salt
1 teaspoon paprika
¼ teaspoon pepper
1 cup bacon drippings
2 cloves of garlic
1 bay leaf
  Milk Gravy (recipe follows)

1 Wash and dry chicken pieces. Shake, a few at a time, in mixture of flour, salt, paprika, and pepper in paper bag to coat well.
2 Heat bacon drippings with whole cloves of garlic and bay leaf in electric skillet, following manufacturer's directions for fried chicken.
3 Place chicken in single layer in hot drippings. (Do not crowd as pieces should have enough room to brown without touching each other.) Cook slowly, turning once or twice to brown both sides. (It will take about 30 minutes.)
4 Return all chicken to skillet; cover; cook slowly 20 minutes, or until tender. Uncover; cook 5 minutes longer to crisp coating. Remove chicken to heated platter; keep hot while making gravy.
  MILK GRAVY—Tip skillet and pour off all drippings into a cup, leaving crusty brown bits in skillet. (Be sure to remove cloves of garlic and bay leaf.) Return 3 tablespoons drippings to skillet; blend in 3 tablespoons flour; cook, stirring all the time, just until mixture bubbles. Stir in 1 cup water and 1 cup milk slowly; continue cooking and stirring, scraping brown bits from bottom and sides of skillet, until gravy thickens and boils 1 minute. Season to taste with salt. Makes about 2 cups.

Dunkin' Chicken

It's finger-food—crackly-crisp outside, juicy all the way through

Makes 6 servings

2 broiler-fryers (about 2 pounds each), cut up
1 cup unsifted all-purpose flour
2 teaspoons salt

½ teaspoon pepper
  Bacon drippings for frying
  Orange-curry Dunk (recipe follows)
  Zippy Tomato Dunk (recipe follows)

1 Wash and dry chicken pieces well. Shake in mixture of flour, salt, and pepper in paper bag to coat well.
2 Heat bacon drippings in large heavy frying pan or electric skillet. It'll take about 1 cup, for fat should be about ½ inch deep. (If you like, use part shortening or vegetable oil.)
3 Place chicken in single layer in hot fat; cover tightly. Cook over *low heat* 20 minutes, or until golden; turn; cover again and cook 20 minutes to brown other side. (If using an electric skillet, follow manufacturer's directions.) Remove browned chicken and set aside while cooking any remaining pieces, adding more drippings, if needed, to keep fat ½ inch deep.
4 Drain fat from frying pan, leaving just enough to keep chicken from sticking; return all chicken to pan. Cover; cook, turning once or twice, over *very low heat* 30 minutes longer, or until chicken is tender.
5 Serve hot or cold, plain or with dunking sauces.

Orange-Curry Dunk

Just sweet, just tart enough to go with mild-flavor chicken.

Makes 2 cups

1 cup orange marmalade
⅓ cup vinegar
¼ cup granulated sugar
2 tablespoons brown sugar
1 tablespoon curry powder
1 tablespoon Worcestershire sauce
1 teaspoon salt
½ teaspoon ground ginger

Combine all ingredients in small saucepan; heat to boiling, then simmer, stirring constantly, until marmalade is melted and sauce is blended. Serve warm or cold.

There are many ways to fry chicken, but few compare with **Country Fried Chicken.**

Zippy Tomato Dunk

It's tomato-rich and spicy—a good all-round sauce to keep on hand

Makes 1½ cups

1 can (8 ounces) tomato sauce
½ cup finely chopped green pepper
½ cup finely chopped celery
2 tablespoons vinegar
2 tablespoons light molasses
1 tablespoon Worcestershire sauce
¼ teaspoon liquid red pepper seasoning

Combine all ingredients in small saucepan; heat to boiling, then simmer, stirring constantly, 5 minutes, or until vegetables are softened and sauce is blended. Serve warm or cold.

Drumstick Fricassee

Lemon-flecked dumpling puffs steam atop meaty chicken legs, sweet potatoes, and peas in rich gravy

Makes 2 servings

4 chicken drumsticks (about 1 pound)
½ small onion, sliced
¼ cup chopped celery tops
1 teaspoon salt
⅛ teaspoon pepper
1½ cups water
2 teaspoons flour
1 large sweet potato, pared and sliced ½ inch thick
1 cup frozen peas (from a 1½-pound bag)
Lemon Dumplings (recipe follows)

Chicken atop a mound of dumplings and vegetables will please everyone as with **Drumstick Fricassee.**

Cook chicken with onion, celery tops, salt, and pepper in 1 cup of the water 30 minutes, or until tender. Blend flour into remaining ½ cup water; stir into broth; cook, stirring constantly, until gravy thickens and boils 1 minute. Add potato and peas; heat to boiling, then simmer 10 minutes while making *Lemon Dumplings*. Drop batter in 4 mounds on top of hot chicken and vegetables; cover tightly. Cook 20 minutes, or until dumplings are fluffy-light. Lift off dumplings; spoon chicken, vegetables, and gravy into serving dishes; top with dumplings. Garnish with grated lemon rind, if you wish.

Lemon Dumplings

Fluffy, light, and fragrant with lemon.

Combine ⅔ cup sifted all-purpose flour, 1 teaspoon baking powder, ½ teaspoon grated lemon rind, and ¼ teaspoon salt. Stir 1 teaspoon lemon juice into ⅓ cup milk. (No need to fuss if mixture curdles.) Add all at once to dry ingredients; stir just until flour mixture is moistened completely.

Jellied Chicken

A perfect make-ahead and wonderful eating on a hot summer day

Makes 6 to 8 servings

1 stewing chicken (5 to 6 pounds), not cut up
1 medium-size onion, sliced
2 teaspoons salt
1 teaspoon peppercorns
 Handful of celery tops
2½ cups water
1 envelope unflavored gelatin
2 hard-cooked eggs, shelled and sliced
 Parsley
1 tablespoon prepared mustard
½ cup dairy sour cream

1 Simmer chicken with onion, salt, peppercorns, celery tops, and water in large kettle, covered, 2 hours, or until tender. Let stand in broth until cool enough to handle.
2 Strain broth into a 4-cup measure; skim off any fat that rises to top, then add water, if needed, to make 3 cups; cool.
3 Pull all chicken from frame; trim off any fat and skin; chop meat fine. (You should have about 4 cups.) Spoon into a 6-cup loaf pan.
4 Soften gelatin in 1 cup of the cooled broth in small saucepan; heat, stirring constantly, just until dissolved. Stir back into remaining broth; pour over chicken in loaf pan, pressing chicken down with a fork until completely covered (mixture should just fill pan).
5 Chill 5 to 6 hours or overnight, or until the loaf is firm enough to cut into neat slices.
6 Unmold onto serving plate; garnish with sliced hard-cooked eggs and parsley. Slice and serve with prepared mustard blended into the sour cream.

Chicken Livers Greek Style

Specially flavored chicken livers combine with tender eggplant for a different dinner idea

Makes 6 servings

1 eggplant (about 1 pound), sliced ½ inch thick
5 tablespoons flour
1 teaspoon salt
2 tablespoons vegetable oil
4 tablespoons (½ stick) butter or margarine
1½ pounds chicken livers, washed and cut in half
1 medium-size onion, sliced
½ teaspoon leaf basil, crumbled
1 can (10¾ ounces) condensed chicken broth
2 tomatoes, peeled and cut in eighths
2 tablespoons chopped parsley

1 Dip eggplant slices in mixture of 3 tablespoons of the flour and salt. Sauté in oil and 2 tablespoons of butter or margarine about 3 minutes on each side, or until soft in a large skillet. Arrange, overlapping, as a border around edge of heated serving dish. Keep warm.
2 Sauté chicken livers and onion in remaining butter or margarine in same skillet 6 minutes, or until browned. Stir in remaining 2 tablespoons flour and basil. Gradually stir in broth.
3 Heat, stirring constantly, until mixture thickens and bubbles 1 minute. Add tomatoes; cover; reduce heat; simmer 5 minutes. Spoon into center of serving dish with eggplant border. Sprinkle with parsley and serve with hot cooked rice, if you wish.

BROILED CHICKEN SAUCES

Garlic-Broiled Chicken: *Warm ½ crushed clove garlic with ¼ cup melted butter or margarine 3 to 5 minutes to mellow flavors; broil chickens as directed, brushing with the garlic butter.*

*   **Lemon-Broiled Chicken:** *Mix the juice of ½ lemon with ¼ cup melted butter or margarine; broil chickens as directed, brushing with the lemon butter.*

*   **Orange-Broiled Chicken:** *Warm 1 to 2 tablespoons tart orange marmalade with ¼ cup melted butter or margarine 3 to 5 minutes; broil chickens as directed, brushing with the orange butter.*

*   **Chili-Broiled Chicken:** *Warm 1 teaspoon chili powder, ½ crushed clove garlic and ⅛ teaspoon cayenne pepper with ¼ cup melted butter or margarine 3 to 5 minutes until no raw chili powder taste remains; broil chickens as directed, brushing with the chili mixture.*

*   **Curry-Broiled Chicken:** *Warm 1 to 2 tablespoons curry powder, ¼ crushed clove garlic and 1 tablespoon finely minced chutney with ¼ cup melted butter or margarine 3 to 5 minutes until no raw curry taste remains; broil chickens as directed, brushing with the curry mixture.*

Basic Broiled Chicken

What could be better or quicker than this simple dish broiled to a crispy brown

Makes 4 servings

2 broiler-fryers (about 2 pounds each), halved or quartered
salt and pepper
¼ cup (½ stick) melted butter or margarine or ¼ cup olive oil or vegetable oil

1 Wash chickens; pat dry. Sprinkle with salt and pepper and brush with melted butter or margarine or with olive or vegetable oil.
2 Place chickens, skin-side down, on rack in broiler pan and broil 6 inches from the heat 20 to 25 minutes, brushing occasionally with the melted butter or margarine or with the oil.
3 Turn chickens, brush with butter, margarine or oil and broil 15 to 20 minutes longer or until nicely browned. *Note:* If chickens brown too quickly, reduce heat or move farther away from broiler unit.

Paella

A tasty melange of chicken and rice that will bring a taste of Spain to your dinner table

Makes 6 servings

1 broiler-fryer, (2½ to 3 pounds), cut up
1 small onion, peeled and sliced
1½ teaspoons salt
   Water
1½ cups uncooked regular rice
2 tablespoons instant minced onion
¼ teaspoon crushed saffron
1 envelope French salad dressing mix
   Vegetable oil
   Cider vinegar
½ head romaine, separated into leaves
2 cans (7 ounces each) minced clams, drained
½ pound salami, cubed
3 medium-size tomatoes, diced
1 jar (6 ounces) marinated artichoke hearts
1 can or jar (4 ounces) pimientos, drained and diced
1 package (10 ounces) frozen peas, cooked and drained
½ cup pitted ripe olives

1 Combine chicken, onion, salt, and 1 cup water in a medium-size frying pan; cover. Simmer 45 minutes, or until chicken is tender. Remove from broth; cool until easy to handle, then pull off skin and take meat from bones; cut into bite-size pieces. Strain broth into a 4-cup measure for next step.
2 Combine rice with instant onion and saffron in a large saucepan; add water to chicken broth to equal amount of liquid called for on rice package; stir into rice. Cook, following label directions. Place in a large bowl.
3 Prepare salad dressing mix with vegetable oil, vinegar, and water, following label directions; fold into rice mixture, then fold in chicken; chill at least an hour to season.
4 When ready to serve, line a large shallow serving dish with romaine.
5 Fold clams, salami, tomatoes, artichoke hearts and liquid, and pimientos into rice mixture; spoon on top of romaine. Spoon peas around edge of rice mixture; tuck olives into peas. Garnish with a large *Pimiento Rose,* if you wish.

PIMIENTO ROSE—Drain liquid from 1 can or jar (4 ounces) whole pimientos. Pat pimientos dry with paper toweling; place on a cutting board. Slit one side of one pimiento from top to bottom and open out flat; roll up tightly, jelly-roll fashion, to form center of rose. Slit remaining pimientos on both sides into two pieces each. Wrap pieces, seed side out and overlapping, around center to form petals.

LEFT-OVER CHICKEN

Deep-Dish Chicken Pie

Not for dieters, but guaranteed to fill up a famished family

Bake at 425° for 30 minutes.
Makes 6 servings

6 medium-size potatoes, pared, quartered
6 medium-size carrots, pared and quartered
1 small onion, chopped (¼ cup)
¼ cup chopped green pepper
2 tablespoons butter or margarine
1 can (10¾ ounces) condensed cream of chicken soup
3 cups chunks of cooked chicken (boiled, roasted, or broiled)
BISCUIT WEDGE TOPPING (recipe follows)

1 Cook potatoes and carrots in boiling salted water in large saucepan 15 to 20 minutes, or until tender; drain, saving 1 cup of liquid for next step.
2 While vegetables cook, sauté onion and green pepper in butter or margarine until soft in saucepan; stir in chicken soup and 1 cup saved liquid.
3 Spoon vegetables and chicken into 8-cup casserole; pour sauce over.
4 Bake in hot oven (425°) 15 minutes while making BISCUIT WEDGE TOPPING; arrange biscuits on top of hot mixture; bake 15 minutes longer, or until biscuits are golden.
BISCUIT WEDGE TOPPING—Sift 1½ cups sifted all-purpose flour, 2 teaspoons baking powder and ½ teaspoon salt into medium-size bowl; cut in ¼ cup (½ stick) butter or margarine; add ½ cup milk all at once; stir just until blended. Turn dough out onto lightly floured pastry cloth or board; knead lightly ½ minute; roll out to a 7-inch round; cut into 6 wedges; brush tops lightly with milk; sprinkle with ¼ teaspoon poppy seeds.

Kashmir Chicken Curry

Freeze this leftover chicken dish, then serve when the family least expects it

Bake at 350° for 2¼ hours.
Makes 4 servings

1 medium-size onion, chopped (½ cup)
1 cup thinly sliced celery
4 tablespoons butter or margarine
2 tablespoons all-purpose flour
2 teaspoons curry powder
1 can (10¾ ounces) condensed chicken broth
Water
1½ teaspoons salt
2½ cups diced cooked chicken
4 cups hot cooked rice (about 1 cup uncooked)

1 To make curry sauce: Sauté onion and celery in butter or margarine until soft in a medium-size saucepan; stir in flour and curry powder. Cook, stirring constantly, until bubbly. Add chicken broth, ½ broth can of water and salt; continue cooking and stirring until mixture thickens and boils 1 minute; remove from heat; add diced cooked chicken.
2 Place hot cooked rice in a large bowl; stir in curry mixture until well blended. Spoon into lightly greased 6-cup freezer-to-oven baking dish.
3 Wrap baking dish tightly with heavy-duty aluminum foil with a double fold on top; seal; label; place in refrigerator until cold; freeze.
4 To heat: Place foil-wrapped, still-frozen curry in cold oven. Set heat at moderate (350°). Bake about 2¼ hours, or until bubbly-hot.

Chicken à la King

Nobody remembers what king this creamy dish is named for, but people have loved it since time immemorial

Makes 4 servings

4 tablespoons (½ stick) butter or margarine
4 tablespoons all-purpose flour
2 tablespoons finely chopped onion
1 teaspoon salt
½ teaspoon Worcestershire sauce
2 cups milk
2 cups diced cooked chicken
¼ cup diced pimiento (about 2 pimientos)
1 can (3 or 4 ounces) sliced mushrooms

(continued)

1 Melt butter or margarine in medium-size saucepan; remove from heat.
2 Blend in flour, onion, salt and Worcestershire sauce; stir in milk.
3 Cook over low heat, stirring constantly, until sauce thickens and boils 1 minute.
4 Stir in chicken, pimiento and mushrooms; heat through.
5 Serve over hot buttered rice or toast, if desired.

Chicken Egg Rolls

This favorite of the Orient goes together so easily at home. For a crisp jacket, fill rolls ahead and chill overnight

Makes 6 servings, 2 rolls each

FILLING

1 large onion, diced (1 cup)
1 cup thinly sliced celery
1 teaspoon vegetable oil
1 tablespoon soy sauce
2 cups diced cooked chicken

PANCAKES

4 eggs
1½ cups water
1½ cups sifted all-purpose flour
1 teaspoon salt
Peanut oil or vegetable oil

1 Make filling: Combine onion, celery and vegetable oil in a small saucepan; cover. Cook over low heat 10 minutes, or until soft. Stir in soy sauce; pour over chicken in a medium-size bowl; toss to mix well. Let stand while making pancakes.
2 Make pancakes: Beat eggs with water until foamy in a medium-size bowl; beat in flour and salt just until smooth. (Batter will be thin.)
3 Heat an 8-inch frying pan slowly; test temperature by sprinkling in a few drops of water. When drops bounce about, temperature is right. Add about 1 teaspoon peanut oil or vegetable oil, tilting pan to cover bottom completely.
4 Pour batter, ¼ cup for each pancake, into pan. Bake 1 to 2 minutes, or until top appears dry and underside is golden. Lift out onto paper toweling to cool. (Only one side is baked.) Repeat with remaining batter, adding a little oil before each baking, to make 12 pancakes; cool each separately on paper toweling.

Chicken Croquettes

When you go to a little trouble with leftover meat, it becomes a whole new dish

Makes 8 croquettes

2 cups coarsely ground cooked chicken
1 cup (about 2 slices) soft bread crumbs
2 eggs, well beaten
2 tablespoons plus ½ cup milk
1 tablespoon minced onion
1 tablespoon minced green pepper
½ teaspoon salt
¼ teaspoon leaf savory, crumbled
* Dash of pepper*
¼ cup finely chopped, blanched, toasted almonds
½ cup fine dry bread crumbs
* Melted vegetable shortening, lard or vegetable oil to make a 3-inch depth in kettle*
SILKY VELOUTÉ SAUCE *(recipe follows)*

1 Combine chicken, soft bread crumbs, eggs, 2 tablespoons milk, onion, green pepper, salt, savory, pepper and almonds in medium-size bowl; chill about 2 hours.
2 Shape into 8 cylindrical croquettes, each 1 inch in diameter; roll in fine dry bread crumbs; dip in ½ cup milk; roll again in crumbs; brush off loose crumbs.
3 Heat fat in deep heavy kettle to 365° or 375° (a 1-inch cube of bread will brown in about 1 minute).
4 Fry croquettes, 2 or 3 at a time, 2 minutes, or until golden-brown; drain on paper toweling.
5 Serve on heated platter with SILKY VELOUTÉ SAUCE.

5 When ready to fill, spoon ¼ cup chicken mixture slightly off center on baked side of each pancake. Fold short end up over filling, then fold both sides toward center and roll up, jelly-roll fashion, to cover filling completely; fasten with one or two wooden picks. Place in a shallow dish; cover; chill overnight.
6 When ready to cook, heat a 1½-inch depth of peanut oil or vegetable oil to 400° in an electric skillet or deep heavy frying pan. Drop in chilled rolls, 2 or 3 at a time; fry, turning once, 5 to 8 minutes, or until golden. Drain on paper toweling. Keep rolls hot in warm oven until all are cooked. Remove picks; serve rolls plain or with a bottled sweet-sour sauce, if you like.

Silky Velouté Sauce

This sauce turns the croquettes into something special

Makes 2 cups sauce

¼ cup (½ stick) butter or margarine
¼ cup sifted all-purpose flour
⅛ teaspoon pepper
1 can (10¾ ounces) condensed chicken broth
¼ cup water
1 teaspoon lemon juice

1 Melt butter or margarine in small saucepan; remove from heat.
2 Blend in flour and pepper; gradually stir in broth and water.
3 Cook over low heat, stirring constantly, until sauce thickens and boils 1 minute; stir in lemon juice. Serve hot.

Pagoda Chicken Bowl

It's a delightfully creamy salad twist on popular chicken and noodles. An instant helper gives you a flying start

Makes 4 servings

1 package (6 ounces) noodles with chicken-sauce mix and almonds
1 can (8¼ ounces) pineapple chunks, drained
1 can (about 9 ounces) pineapple tidbits, drained
1 cup sliced celery
2 cups cubed cooked chicken
⅓ cup mayonnaise or salad dressing
¼ cup milk
¼ teaspoon curry powder
Boston lettuce
Radish slices

1 Prepare noodles with chicken-sauce mix, following label directions for top-range method; set almonds aside for Step 3. Spoon noodle mixture into a medium-size bowl; cool, stirring lightly several times, at room temperature.
2 Set aside several pineapple chunks and celery slices for a garnish; stir remaining pineapple and chicken into noodle mixture. Blend mayonnaise or salad dressing, milk and curry powder in a cup; fold into noodle mixture. Chill at least 30 minutes to season.
3 When ready to serve, spoon into a lettuce-lined salad bowl; sprinkle saved almonds on top. Garnish with rows of radish slices and saved pineapple chunks and celery threaded on a wooden pick.

Curried Chicken Leftover

This one is a whole meal in itself. Almonds and apple add texture

Makes 4 servings

¾ cup precooked rice
½ cup chopped red apple
1 cup diced cooked chicken
¼ cup toasted slivered almonds
1½ teaspoons grated onion
⅓ cup mayonnaise or salad dressing
2 tablespoons table cream or light cream
1 tablespoon lemon juice
½ teaspoon curry powder
¼ teaspoon salt
¼ teaspoon sugar

1 Cook rice in a small saucepan, following label directions; cool to room temperature. Combine with apple, chicken, almonds and onion in a medium-size bowl.
2 Blend remaining ingredients in a cup; stir into rice mixture; chill. Just before serving, garnish with red apple slices, if you wish.

When you feel that a foreign meal is in order try one of these bountiful trios: **London Turkey Pie, Indonesian Rijsttafel,** and **Parmiagiana Chicken Cutlets** (see Chicken section).

Let Turkey Do The Work

Imagine Thanksgiving without turkey! Better yet, imagine turkey year-round. And this is possible today. With the exciting recipes on these pages, you'll find every day is the right day for turkey—stewed, roasted, or using one of your favorite cooking methods.

ALL-OCCASION TURKEY RECIPES

Indonesian Rijsttafel

This is literally a "rice table" for the satays, or kabobs of pungent turkey cubes that are surrounded with deep-fried sweet potato

Makes 4 servings.

3 cups cubed cooked turkey
½ cup orange marmalade
¼ cup lime juice
¼ teaspoon bottled red pepper seasoning
 FRIED RICE (recipe follows)
 SWEET POTATO CRISPS (see recipe in this section)

1 Thread turkey cubes onto 4 wooden skewers. Combine marmalade, lime juice and bottled red pepper seasoning in a cup; brush over turkey.
2 Preheat portable electric broiler, following manufacturer's directions. Broil kabobs, turning often and brushing with remaining glaze, 10 minutes, or until golden.
3 Spoon FRIED RICE onto a heated serving platter; arrange kabobs on rice; sprinkle *Sweet Potato Crisps* around.

Fried Rice

The rice goes with the Indonesian Rijsttafel

Makes 4 servings.

3 tablespoons vegetable oil
1 cup sliced green onions
1 cup finely diced cooked ham
4 cups cooked rice (1 cup uncooked)

2 tablespoons soy sauce
 Dash cayenne pepper

1 Heat oil in an electric frypan set at 375°; sauté green onions in oil until soft; stir in ham and cook 2 minutes.
2 Stir in rice, soy sauce and cayenne pepper until well blended; lower heat control to 200°; cover frypan; cook 15 minutes, or until rice is piping-hot.

London Turkey Pie

Pie birds are a traditional touch to meat pies in Great Britain: you can make this recipe without it, but it won't be as much fun

Bake at 400° for 20 minutes.
Makes 4 servings.

1 can (10¾ ounces) condensed cream of
 onion soup
¼ cup light cream or milk
1 teaspoon Worcestershire sauce
1 can (1 pound) mixed vegetables, drained
2 cups diced cooked turkey
1 teaspoon leaf savory, crumbled
1¼ cups sifted all-purpose flour
½ teaspoon salt
⅓ cup vegetable shortening
3 tablespoons cold water
1 egg yolk

1 Combine soup, cream or milk and Worcestershire sauce in a large saucepan; bring to boiling; lower heat; stir in vegetables, turkey and savory; simmer while making pastry.
2 Sift flour and salt into a medium-size bowl; cut in shortening with a pastry blender until mixture is crumbly; stir in water with a fork, just until mixture leaves the side of bowl; pack into ball on wax paper.
3 Turn out dough onto a lightly floured pastry cloth or board; roll out to a ½-inch thick oval or round (match shape of casserole).
4 Invert casserole onto pastry and cut pastry ½-inch wider than dish; make a hole in center of pastry for pie bird base. (Or make several slits in pastry, if not using pie bird.)
5 Place pie bird base in center of casserole; spoon hot turkey mixture into dish; lift pastry

(continued)

from cloth or board to casserole with rolling pin, putting hole over pie bird base; press pastry against side of casserole.

6 Beat egg yolk with a few drops water in a cup; brush over pastry with a soft brush. Cut pastry trims into leaves with paring knife; arrange on pastry; brush with egg mixture.

7 Preheat portable electric oven to hot (400°).

8 Bake pie for 20 minutes, or until crust is golden. Insert pie bird into base before serving.

Basic Roast Turkey

It may be called basic, but this is a succulent dish that everyone will enjoy

Roast at 325° from 4 to 4½ hours.
Makes 12 servings

1 cleaned fresh or frozen turkey (about 12 to 14 pounds)
Salt (plain or seasoned)
12 cups any favorite poultry stuffing (see Some Favorite Poultry Stuffings that follow)
6 tablespoons (¾ stick) butter or margarine, melted

1 Sprinkle inside of bird lightly with plain or seasoned salt, then lightly stuff neck cavity. Smooth neck skin over stuffing and skewer to back of bird. Twist wing tips until they rest flat against skewered neck skin.

2 Stuff body cavity, taking care not to pack the stuffing (it needs room to expand as it cooks). If turkey comes "tucked" (with legs slipped under a ribbon-like skin band across opening), slide legs out, stuff lightly, then slip legs back in place. If turkey is not a "tucked" type, lace opening together with poultry pins or skewers and string and truss legs close to body.

3 Brush stuffed bird all over with melted butter or margarine, place, breast-side up, in roasting pan—on a rack, if you wish—but do not cover pan or add any water. If using a meat thermometer, stick it into the center of a thigh without touching bone.

4 Roast in a slow oven (325°) for time suggested on turkey wrapper or about 4 hours for a 12-pounder or until thermometer registers 185°. After bird has been in the oven about 30 minutes, brush again with melted butter. During rest of roasting time, baste every half hour with buttery drippings in pan.

5 Start testing for doneness 30 minutes before roasting time is up. Protecting your fingers with paper toweling, squeeze meaty part of thigh.

It should feel soft. Now move drumstick up and down. It should twist and move easily.

6 When turkey is done, remove strings and skewers, place on a heated platter and keep warm while making *Giblet Gravy* or *Onion-Mushroom Gravy* (both recipes are included in this section) or your own favorite gravy.

Note: Turkey will carve more neatly if allowed to stand 15 to 20 minutes beforehand.

Golden Twin Turkeys

Wrap what you don't eat now and have a delicious family meal later

Roast at 325° about 2½ hours.
Makes 8 servings,
plus enough for another meal

2 cleaned fresh or frozen turkeys (about 6 pounds each)
Salt
8 cups any favorite poultry stuffing or 4 cups each of 2 different stuffings (see Some Favorite Poultry Stuffings that follow)
1 can (10½ ounces) condensed beef broth
½ cup (1 stick) butter or margarine

1 Sprinkle insides of birds with salt, then lightly stuff neck cavities. Smooth neck skins over stuffing and skewer to backs of birds. Twist wing tips until they rest flat against skewered neck skins.

2 Stuff body cavities, taking care not to pack the stuffing. If turkeys come "tucked" (with legs slipped under a ribbon-like skin band across opening), slide legs out, stuff lightly, then slip legs back in place. If turkeys are not the "tucked" type, lace openings together with poultry pins or skewers and string and truss legs close to bodies.

3 Place birds, breast-side up and side by side, not touching, on a rack in a large roasting pan. Do not cover pan or add any water. Insert meat thermometer into the thickest part of a thigh without touching bone.

4 Heat beef broth and butter or margarine in a small saucepan just until butter or margarine melts. Brush part over turkeys to coat well.

5 Roast turkeys in a slow oven (325°), brushing every half hour with remaining broth mixture, 2½ hours, or until thermometer registers 185°.

6 Start testing for doneness 30 minutes before roasting time is up. Protecting your fingers with paper toweling, squeeze the meaty part of a

(continued)

When the meal calls for tradition, serve **Basic Roast Turkey** accompanied by all the trimmings.

thigh. It should feel soft. Now move a drumstick up and down. It should twist and move easily.
7 When turkeys are done, remove strings and skewers, place on a heated serving platter and let stand 15 to 20 minutes before carving. *Note:* This is a good time to make gravy—*Giblet or Onion-Mushroom Gravy* (both recipes are included in this section) or your own favorite gravy.

Cranberry-Glazed Roast Turkey

Pop a frozen ready-stuffed bird into a pan, roast, and glaze—it's that simple

Roast at 325° about 6 hours.
Makes 8 servings,
plus enough for another meal

1 frozen stuffed turkey (about 10 pounds)
½ cup (1 stick) butter or margarine, softened
1 can (7 ounces) jellied cranberry sauce
1 teaspoon Worcestershire sauce
½ teaspoon leaf marjoram, crumbled

1 Remove frozen stuffed turkey from wrapper; place turkey, breast up, on a rack in a roasting pan; coat with soft butter or margarine.
2 Roast, following label directions for turkey cooked in an uncovered pan, and basting every hour with buttery drippings in pan, 5½ hours.
3 Pour off all drippings into a small bowl; measure 2 tablespoonfuls into a small saucepan; set remaining aside for making gravy, if you wish.
4 Stir cranberry and Worcestershire sauces and marjoram into drippings in saucepan; heat, stirring constantly, just to boiling. Brush part over turkey.
5 Continue roasting, basting several times with remaining cranberry mixture, 30 minutes longer, or until drumstick feels very soft and a meat thermometer inserted into center of stuffing registers 165°.
6 Remove turkey to a heated platter; carve and serve. After serving, remove any leftover stuffing from turkey and chill separately.
    NOTE—If you wish to make gravy, fix it in another pan, as the cranberry drippings in the roasting pan tend to make the gravy too sweet.

Roast Turkey Breast With Chestnut Stuffing

Your basic turkey roast with a delicious stuffing that's sure to please

Roast at 325° for 2½ hours.
Makes about 8 servings

1 medium-size onion, chopped
½ cup diced celery
½ cup (1 stick) butter or margarine
1 tablespoon parsley flakes
1½ teaspoons leaf thyme, crumbled
1 teaspoon salt
¼ teaspoon pepper
1 cup coarsely chopped canned chestnuts
⅓ cup water
6 slices white bread, toasted and cut in tiny cubes (3 cups)
1 frozen turkey breast (about 5 pounds), thawed

1 Sauté onion and celery in ¼ cup of the butter or margarine until soft in a medium-size frying pan. Stir in parsley, thyme, salt, pepper, chestnuts, and water; heat to boiling. Pour over bread in a large bowl; toss until evenly moist.
2 Turn turkey breast upside down on a cutting board; spread open. Lightly stuff chestnut mixture into neck and breast cavities. Fold sides of breast up over stuffing; hold in place with skewers. Smooth neck skin over stuffing; skewer. Place roast, skin side up, on a rack in a shallow roasting pan.
3 Melt remaining ¼ cup butter or margarine in a small saucepan; brush over turkey. Insert meat thermometer into thickest part of breast without touching bone. Cover pan loosely with foil.
4 Roast in slow oven (325°) 1½ hours; uncover. Continue roasting, brushing turkey several times with drippings in pan, 1 hour longer, or until turkey is tender and thermometer registers 185°
5 Place turkey on a heated serving platter; remove skewers. Surround with sautéed mushrooms and buttered whole green beans, if you wish.

Giblet Gravy

With broth ready ahead of time, gravy goes together quickly

Makes about 4 cups

Turkey giblets (except liver and neck)
1 medium-size onion, chopped

Few celery tops
1 teaspoon salt
1 bay leaf
4 cups water
Turkey liver
8 tablespoons turkey fat
½ cup sifted all-purpose flour
Salt and pepper to season

1 Combine giblets, onion, celery tops, 1 teaspoon salt, bay leaf and 4 cups water in a medium-size saucepan. Simmer 1 hour and 40 minutes; add liver, simmer 20 minutes longer or until meat is tender.
2 Strain broth; measure; add water, if necessary, to make 4 cups.
3 Chop giblets fine and stir into broth. Cool, then chill until ready to make gravy.
4 After turkey has been removed from roasting pan, remove rack, if used; tip pan and let fat rise in one corner. Pour all fat into a cup leaving juices in pan. Measure 8 tablespoons fat and return to pan; blend in flour. Cook, stirring constantly, just until bubbly.
5 Stir in 4 cups giblet broth and giblets; continue cooking and stirring, scraping baked-on juices from bottom and sides of pan, until gravy thickens and boils 1 minute.
6 Season to taste with salt and pepper; stir in a little bottled gravy coloring to darken, if you wish.

Onion-Mushroom Gravy

Onion soup mix richens the savory broth for this variation of a holiday-dinner must

Makes about 4 cups

Turkey giblets
1 bay leaf
3½ cups water
1 envelope onion soup mix
8 tablespoons turkey drippings
½ cup sifted all-purpose flour
1 can (6 ounces) sliced mushrooms

1 Combine turkey giblets (except liver) and necks with bay leaf and water in a medium-size saucepan. Heat to boiling; stir in soup mix.
2 Simmer 40 minutes; add livers. Simmer 20 minutes longer, or until giblets are tender. Remove from broth and chill to dice for soup for another day. Measure broth and add water, if needed, to make 3½ cups.
3 After turkeys have been removed from roast-

ing pan, remove rack, if used. Tip pan and let drippings rise in one corner, then pour off into a cup, leaving juices in pan. Measure the 8 tablespoons drippings and return to pan.
4 Blend in flour; cook, stirring constantly, until bubbly. Stir in the 3½ cups broth and mushrooms and liquid. Continue cooking and stirring, scraping baked-on juices from bottom and sides of pan, until gravy thickens and boils 1 minute. Stir in a few drops bottled gravy coloring to darken, if you wish, and season with salt and pepper, if needed.

TURKEY ROASTING CHART			
	Ready-to-Cook Weight	Oven Temp.	Guide to Roasting Time
Turkey	6-8 lbs.	325°	3½-4 hrs.
	8-12 lbs.	325°	4-4½ hrs.
	12-16 lbs.	325°	4½-5½ hrs.
	16-20 lbs.	325°	5½-6½ hrs.
	20-24 lbs.	325°	6½-7½ hrs.
Foil-Wrapped Turkey	7-9 lbs.	450°	2¼-2½ hrs.
	10-13 lbs.	450°	2¾-3 hrs.
	14-17 lbs.	450°	3-3¼ hrs.
	18-21 lbs.	450°	3¼-3½ hrs.
	22-24 lbs.	450°	3¼-3¾ hrs.

Dutch-Oven Turkey

Practical platter: Handy two-pound frozen roast, macaroni, and vegetables

Makes 6 servings

1 packaged frozen boneless turkey roast, (about 2 pounds)
2 tablespoons vegetable oil
½ teaspoon monosodium glutamate
½ teaspoon seasoned salt
¼ teaspoon seasoned pepper
1 envelope instant beef broth
 OR: 1 beef bouillon cube
1 medium-size onion, chopped (½ cup)
1 cup water
1 can (1 pound) cut green beans
2 cups thinly sliced celery
1 cup uncooked elbow macaroni

1 Remove turkey roast from foil package Brown slowly in vegetable oil in a Dutch oven or electric skillet.

(continued)

2 Stir in monosodium glutamate, seasoned salt and pepper, beef broth or bouillon cube, onion, and water. Heat to boiling; cover.

3 Simmer, turning meat once or twice, 2 hours, or until tender. Remove to a cutting board; keep warm while cooking vegetables and macaroni.

4 Pour liquid from Dutch oven into a 4-cup measure; drain liquid from green beans into same cup. Add water, if needed, to make 4 cups. Return to Dutch oven; heat to boiling.

5 Stir in celery, macaroni, and beans. Cook, stirring several times, 10 minutes, or until macaroni and celery are tender and almost all of the liquid has evaporated. Spoon vegetables onto a heated large deep platter.

6 Carve turkey into ¼-inch-thick slices; arrange, overlapping, over vegetables. Sprinkle lightly with chopped parsley, if you wish.

Turkey Platter Indienne

Buy one of the new about-two-pound boneless turkey roasts to cook, slice, and glaze for this easy curry-style dinner

Roast at 400° for 2 hours, then bake at 350° for 15 minutes.

Makes 8 servings

1 packaged frozen boneless turkey roast (about 2 pounds)
½ cup apricot preserves (from a 12-ounce jar)
¼ cup apple cider
1 teaspoon curry powder
  Herbed Pilaf (recipe follows)
  Sweet-potato Crispies (recipe follows)

What better feast than **Dutch-Oven Turkey,** complete with cranberry sauce and pumpkin pie.

Golden Spiced Peaches (recipe follows)
Sautéed Cucumber Wedges (recipe follows)
Chopped radishes and green onions

1 Roast frozen turkey in its foil package, following label directions; remove from package; cool. (Meat slices more neatly if allowed to cool first. Or roast turkey a day ahead and keep chilled until ready to finish dish.)
2 Cut turkey into 24 thin slices; place in a single layer in a jelly-roll pan, 15x10x1.
3 Mix apricot preserves, cider, and curry powder in a small saucepan; heat, stirring constantly, until preserves melt and sauce is hot; brush over turkey slices.
4 Bake in moderate oven (350°) 15 minutes, or until turkey is heated through and richly glazed.
5 Spoon *Herbed Pilaf* onto a large serving platter, mounding it in center; arrange turkey slices, overlapping, in a ring on top. Garnish with a preserved kumquat flower, if you wish. (To make, cut a preserved kumquat into eighths from tip almost to stem end; separate petals slightly; stuff with a sprig of parsley.)
6 Serve with little bowls of *Sweet-Potato Crispies, Golden Spiced Peaches, Sautéed Cucumber Wedges,* and chopped radishes and green onions to sprinkle on top.

Herbed Pilaf

Pan-toasted rice and bulgur wheat make this delectable go-with for curried turkey

Makes 8 servings

1 cup uncooked regular rice
¼ cup peanut oil or vegetable oil
1 large onion, chopped (1 cup)
1 cup chopped celery
4 envelopes instant chicken broth
  OR: 4 chicken bouillon cubes
1 teaspoon leaf rosemary, crumbled
4 cups water
1 cup bulgur wheat or wheat pilaf (from a 1-pound package)

1 Sauté rice, stirring constantly, in peanut oil or vegetable oil until toasty-golden in a large frying pan; remove with a slotted spoon and set aside. Stir onion and celery into drippings in pan; sauté just until soft.
2 Stir in chicken broth or bouillon cubes, rosemary, and water; heat to boiling, crushing cubes, if using, with a spoon. Stir in bulgur wheat and browned rice; cover.

3 Simmer, stirring once or twice, 1 hour, or until liquid is absorbed and wheat and rice are fluffy-tender.

Sweet-Potato Crispies

Just a few sprinkled over the turkey and pilaf add a pleasingly crunchy contrast.

Makes 8 servings

2 large sweet potatoes
  Shortening or vegetable oil for frying

1 Pare sweet potatoes, then shred finely; pat dry on paper toweling.
2 Melt enough shortening or pour in enough vegetable oil to make a 2-inch depth in a small saucepan; heat to 350°
3 Fry shredded potatoes, a heaping tablespoonful at a time, 1 to 2 minutes or until crisp. Lift out with a slotted spoon; drain well on paper toweling. Serve warm.

Golden Spiced Peaches

Jiffy-quick to fix and so good with turkey.

Makes 8 servings

1 can (1 pound) cling peach slices
1 tablespoon mixed pickling spices

1 Drain syrup from peaches into a small saucepan; stir in pickling spices. Heat to boiling, then simmer 5 minutes.
2 While syrup heats, cut each peach slice into thirds; place in a small bowl.
3 Strain syrup over peaches; cover; chill several hours to blend flavors.

Sautéed Cucumber Wedges

This popular vegetable is heated just long enough to take on a buttery-rich coating

Makes 8 servings

2 large cucumbers
2 tablespoons butter or margarine

1 Pare cucumbers; quarter each lengthwise, then cut into ½-inch wedges.
2 Sauté in butter or margarine just until hot in a medium-size frying pan. Serve warm.

TYPES OF TURKEY

Fryer-Roasters: Small meaty turkeys weighing from 4 to 9 pounds:
  Roasters: These range in size from about 10 to 30 pounds for a Banquet Tom. The advantage of substituting two small birds for one giant is that you double the number of drumsticks, thighs, wings and breasts. The disadvantage is that small birds may not look quite so festive on the groaning board.
  Boneless Turkey Roasts: Plump roasts weighing from 2 to 8 pounds.
  Turkey Parts: Turkey drumsticks, wings, thighs and sometimes breasts are beginning to be marketed the way chicken parts are. The legs and wings, particularly, offer good eating at relatively low cost.
  Frozen Pre-Stuffed Turkeys: Available in a broad range of sizes from small "junior" turkeys to near 20 pounders. Most popular are those in the 8 to 12 pound class.
  Frozen Self-Basting Turkeys: Injected with butter before being frozen, these turkeys do actually baste themselves as they cook, taking a lot of the drudgery out of the job. They are available in a wide range of sizes.
  Frozen Boneless Turkey Rolls: These are available raw, fully cooked or smoked, as all dark or all white meat or combinations of the two. Weights range from 3 to 10 pounds.
  Frozen Turkey Steaks: Turkey minute steaks, available plain and breaded.
  Smoked Turkey: A gourmet item, ready to slice and eat.

Turkey Roast Royale

The elegant apricot stuffing makes this a bird fit for a king

Roast at 350° about 2½ hours.
Makes 8 servings,
plus enough for a bonus meal

1 frozen boneless white-and-dark-meat turkey roast (about 4½ pounds)
¼ teaspoon seasoned salt
¼ teaspoon pepper
3 tablespoons butter or margarine
1 cup dry white wine

2 tablespoons flour
¼ cup water
  Apricot Stuffing (recipe follows)

1 Thaw turkey roast, following label directions; remove from wrapper or carton. Place roast, skin-side up, on a rack in a small roasting pan; sprinkle with salt and pepper. Insert meat thermometer into roast so bulb reaches center.
2 Melt butter or margarine in a small saucepan; stir in wine. Pour over roast; cover.
3 Roast in moderate oven (350°), spooning liquid in pan over roast several times, 1½ hours; uncover.
4 Continue roasting 1 hour, or until thermometer registers 185° and roast is lightly browned. Remove roast from pan; keep warm while making gravy.
5 Pour liquid from pan into a 1-cup measure; add water or dry white wine, if needed, to make 1 cup. Return to pan; heat to boiling.
6 Smooth flour and the ¼ cup water to a paste in a cup; stir into boiling liquid. Cook, stirring constantly, until gravy thickens and boils 1 minute. Season with salt and pepper, if needed.
7 Place roast on a heated large serving platter; spoon *Apricot Stuffing* around edge. Garnish with canned apricot halves stuffed with pecans, and parsley, if you wish. Slice roast, removing strings as you go; serve gravy separately.

Apricot Stuffing

A stuffing fit for Turkey Roast Royale

Bake at 350° for 1 hour.
Makes 8 servings

1 cup dried apricots, chopped
1½ cups water
1 cup diced celery
½ cup (1 stick) butter or margarine
1 envelope instant chicken broth or 1 teaspoon granulated chicken bouillon
1 cup chopped pecans
1 teaspoon salt
12 slices white bread, toasted and cut in tiny cubes (6 cups)

1 Heat apricots and ½ cup of the water to boiling in a small saucepan; remove from heat. Let stand about 10 minutes.
2 Sauté celery in butter or margarine until soft in a medium-size frying pan; stir in remaining 1 cup water, chicken broth, pecans, and salt. Heat to boiling.

There's no problem with slicing when you start off with the frozen boneless turkey roast used for **Turkey Roast Royale.**

When the roast turkey is hot, carve off eight slices for fanciful **Turkey Alfredo.**

3 Place bread cubes in a large bowl; spoon apricot and celery mixtures over top; toss lightly until evenly moist. Spoon into an 8-cup baking dish; cover.
4 Bake in moderate oven (350°) 1 hour.

Turkey Alfredo

Cheese-seasoned noodles, breaded and browned slices of cooked turkey, and a rich saucy topping make this Continental treat

Makes 4 servings

1 package (8 ounces) regular noodles
1 cup freshly grated Parmesan cheese
½ cup (1 stick) butter or margarine
    Supreme Sauce (recipe follows)
1 egg
1 teaspoon leaf oregano, crumbled
½ teaspoon salt
    Dash of pepper
2 tablespoons water
¾ cup fine dry bread crumbs
8 slices roast breast of turkey
3 tablespoons olive oil or vegetable oil

1 Cook noodles in a kettle, following label directions; drain; return to kettle. Add Parmesan cheese and 5 tablespoons of the butter or margarine; toss lightly with two forks until butter or margarine melts and noodles are evenly coated. Keep hot. (Remaining butter or margarine is for Step 4.)
2 While noodles cook, make *Supreme Sauce*; set aside for Step 5.
3 Beat egg with oregano, salt, pepper, and water in a pie plate; place bread crumbs in a second pie plate.
4 Dip turkey slices into egg mixture, then into bread crumbs to coat well. Brown slices, a few at a time, in the remaining 3 tablespoons butter or margarine mixed with olive oil or vegetable oil in a large frying pan.
5 Spoon hot noodles into an 8-cup shallow broilerproof dish; arrange turkey slices, overlapping, on top; spoon *Supreme Sauce* over middle of turkey slices.
6 Broil, 4 inches from heat, 5 minutes, or until sauce puffs and turns golden.

Supreme Sauce

Whipped cream folded into the sauce adds the gourmet touch.

Makes about ¾ cup

2 tablespoons butter or margarine
2 tablespoons flour
1 envelope instant chicken broth
    OR: 1 chicken bouillon cube
½ cup milk
¼ cup cream for whipping

1 Melt butter or margarine in a small saucepan; stir in flour and chicken broth or bouillon cube. Cook, stirring constantly and crushing cube, if using, with a spoon, just until bubbly.
2 Stir in milk; continue cooking and stirring until sauce thickens and boils 1 minute; remove from heat.
3 Beat cream until stiff in a small bowl; fold into sauce.

HOW MUCH TURKEY TO BUY

When buying turkeys under 12 pounds, allow ¾ to 1 pound per serving; when buying birds weighing more than 12 pounds, allow ½ to ¾ pound per serving (there is proportionately more meat on the big birds).

Drumstick Dinner

A beautiful and unusual way to serve this economical food

Bake at 375° for 40 minutes.
Makes 4 servings

4 frozen turkey drumsticks, (about 1 pound each), thawed
2 tablespoons vegetable oil
1 large onion, chopped (1 cup)
1 teaspoon salt
¼ teaspoon pepper
1 can (13¾ ounces) chicken broth
½ cup ginger marmalade (from a 12-ounce jar)
⅓ cup light molasses
⅓ cup cider vinegar
⅓ cup prepared mustard
1 teaspoon ground ginger
    Tangerine Risotto (recipe follows)

(continued)

1 Brown drumsticks slowly in vegetable oil in a large frying pan; remove from pan.
2 Stir onion into drippings; sauté until soft. Stir in salt, pepper, and chicken broth; heat to boiling. Place drumsticks in sauce; cover. Simmer, turning several times, 1½ hours, or until tender. Remove drumsticks from pan and place on a rack in a shallow baking pan.
3 Blend marmalade, molasses, vinegar, mustard, and ginger in a small saucepan; heat slowly to boiling. Brush part over drumsticks.
4 Bake in moderate oven (375°), turning and brushing several times with remaining molasses mixture, 40 minutes, or until richly glazed.
5 Spoon *Tangerine Risotto* onto a heated large serving platter; arrange turkey drumsticks, spoke fashion, on top. Garnish platter with parsley and small cubes of jellied cranberry sauce, if you wish.

Tangerine Risotto

Served with Drumstick Dinner, this makes a festive meal

Makes 4 servings

1 cup uncooked regular rice
4 tablespoons (½ stick) butter or margarine
1 medium-size seedless orange
1 large onion, chopped (1 cup)
⅓ cup thawed frozen concentrated tangerine juice
1 can (5 ounces) water chestnuts, drained and sliced
1 teaspoon sugar
½ teaspoon salt

1 Cook rice in a large saucepan, following label directions. Stir in 2 tablespoons of the butter or margarine; keep warm.
2 While rice cooks, pare orange; section over a small bowl to catch the juice; cut each section in half.
3 Sauté onion in remaining 2 tablespoons butter or margarine until soft in a medium-size frying pan; stir in orange sections and juice, concentrated tangerine juice, water chestnuts, sugar, and salt. Heat slowly to boiling.
4 Pour over rice mixture; toss lightly to mix.

HOW TO USE TURKEY CUTLETS OR SCALOPPINE

Turkey scaloppine or cutlets, cut from the white breast meat, are ringers for those of the classic veal and cost about one-fifth of the price. As with veal, the cutlets are thinly sliced, then pounded in order to break the connective tissue that would tighten when heated.

Cutlets should be the first use made of breast meat, so you have the largest, choicest white meat for them. As you work closer to the breastbone, pieces become smaller and are more suited to ground recipes. To prepare cutlets, make a sharp cut down one side of the breastbone, through both skin and flesh. Remove skin from one or both breasts, depending on how many cutlets you will need, and carefully pull off the thin covering membrane from the top of the breast meat.

Next, positioning the turkey as you would for slicing, place your left hand on the breast meat to hold it firm and, using a very sharp, thin-bladed knife, slice across the breast to make a tapered, palm-shaped slice, about one-third of an inch thick. Trim off any opaque white membrane or connective tissue from the edges of the slices.

Working on a cutting board, place each slice of turkey between two sheets of wax paper. Using a flat-sided mallet or tenderizer (nothing scored or ridged will do), pound the turkey cutlet to about one-quarter-inch thickness, being careful not to pound so hard you mash or tear it. If you have no mallet, pound the cutlet with the flat underside of a small, heavy saucepan or skillet. If cutlets are made in advance of their actual use, leave them between the sheets of wax paper and freeze. Prepared that way and well wrapped in freezer paper, you can also be sure that they are thoroughly thawed before beginning any of the preparations.

It is best to use a large turkey for cutlets as that makes it possible to have wider, more perfect slices. In order to obtain 8 to 10 large cutlets, use a turkey 18 pounds or larger. A 12- to 15-pound turkey will provide 6 to 8 decent-size slices.

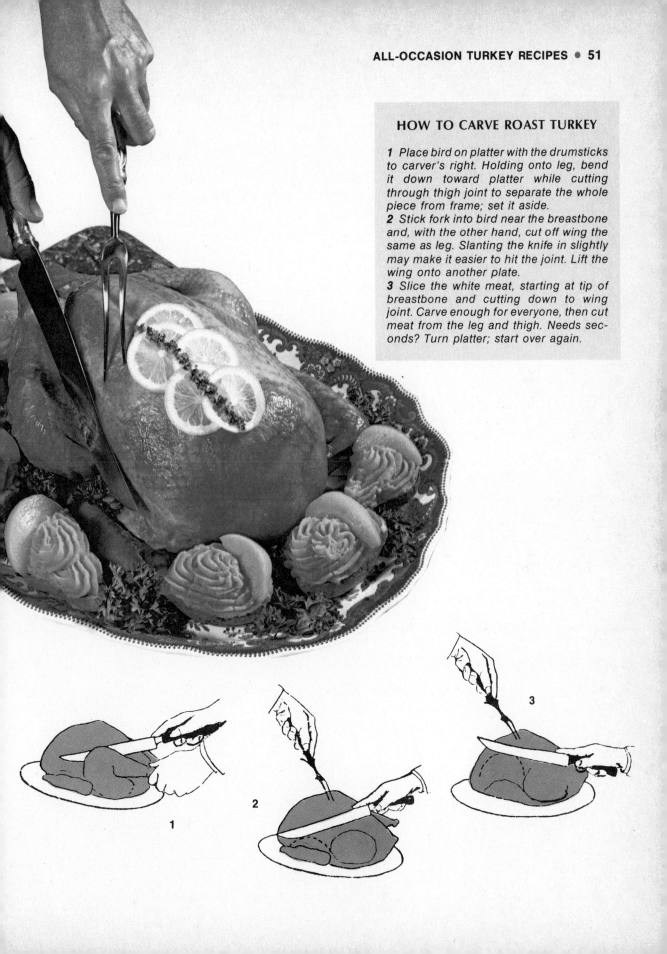

HOW TO CARVE ROAST TURKEY

1 Place bird on platter with the drumsticks to carver's right. Holding onto leg, bend it down toward platter while cutting through thigh joint to separate the whole piece from frame; set it aside.

2 Stick fork into bird near the breastbone and, with the other hand, cut off wing the same as leg. Slanting the knife in slightly may make it easier to hit the joint. Lift the wing onto another plate.

3 Slice the white meat, starting at tip of breastbone and cutting down to wing joint. Carve enough for everyone, then cut meat from the leg and thigh. Needs seconds? Turn platter; start over again.

1

2

3

Turkey Cutlets Bolognese

While turkey is really a substitute for veal in some of the other dishes, in this recipe it is the authentic ingredient

Makes 8 servings.

8 turkey cutlets, each about 4x3 inches
   (2 pounds)
1 teaspoon salt
½ teaspoon black pepper
7 tablespoons butter
3 tablespoons vegetable oil
¾ cup flour, for dredging
½ pound large mushrooms
½ cup Marsala or dry Vermouth
¼ pound prosciutto, thinly sliced OR:
8 slices bacon, partially cooked
3 tablespoons grated Parmesan cheese
¼ pound Fontina or Swiss cheese, coarsely
   grated or slivered

1 Pound cutlets as directed; dry with paper toweling. Sprinkle one side of each cutlet with salt and pepper.

Thinly sliced and pounded, turkey-breast meat makes tender scalopping. Baked with cheese and ham in **Turkey Cutlets Bolognese,** it is the classic ingredient.

2 Heat 4 tablespoons butter with oil and, as they heat, dredge cutlets lightly on both sides with flour. When frying foam subsides, add cutlets, a few at a time and quickly fry until light golden brown on both sides. This should take no more than 4 minutes for each batch. Keep fried cutlets warm while remainder are browned.

3 If mushrooms are sandy, wash under running cold water and dry well. If not, just rub with a clean towel. Using caps only (reserve stems for soup or gravy) slice thinly.

4 Heat remaining 3 tablespoons butter in another pan and quickly sauté sliced mushrooms until they have golden brown edges. Pour Marsala into mushroom pan, simmer for a minute or two, then pour into the pan in which cutlets were fried. Simmer again, scraping coagulated pan juices into the wine.

5 Lightly cover the bottom of an open baking pan with some of the pan juices (about 2 tablespoons) and lay cutlets on bottom, overlapping slightly. Top each with a slice of prosciutto or bacon then with a row of the sautéed mushrooms and a sprinkling of Parmesan. Top with Fontina or Swiss and pour on the rest of the sauce in the skillet.

6 Place in a hot oven (425°) and bake for 5 to 8 minutes, or until cheese is bubbling hot. This is especially good with rice cooked in chicken stock and butter and creamed spinach.

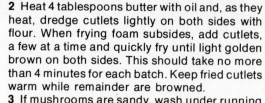

If you follow the directions properly, your roast turkey can be carved as neatly as this one.

Scaloppine Milanese

Fried Cutlets with a delightful cheese flavor

Makes 6 servings.

6 turkey cutlets, each about 4x3-inches
    (2 pounds)
1 teaspoon salt
½ teaspoon black pepper
2 eggs lightly beaten with
2 tablespoons olive or vegetable oil
    Flour for dredging
    Packaged bread crumbs for coating
    Vegetable oil for frying

1 Pound cutlets as directed; pat dry with paper toweling. Season one side of each cutlet with sprinklings of salt and pepper. Dredge lightly with flour. Dip in beaten egg, letting excess drip off.
2 Dredge cutlets in crumbs. If you like, season bread crumbs by tossing in a little grated Parmesan cheese—about 2 tablespoons of cheese per cup of bread crumbs; chill, uncovered, in refrigerator for 10 to 30 minutes.
3 In a large, heavy skillet, heat a one-inch depth of olive or vegetable oil to about 375 degrees. Fry cutlets, a few at a time (they should not touch in the pan), until golden brown on first side. Turn and brown second side. Total frying time should be about 8 minutes.
4 Drain on paper towel and keep warm in low oven until all are fried. Serve with lemon wedges.

Turkey Cutlets Cordon Bleu

Don't be mislead by the title; these cutlets are easy to prepare

Makes 4 servings.

4 large or 8 small turkey cutlets, prepared as
    above
1 teaspoon salt (about)
½ teaspoon black pepper (about)
½ pound mozzarella cheese (sliced and
    shaped to size of cutlets)
2 ounces thinly sliced prosciutto (optional)
2 eggs, lightly beaten with
2 tablespoons cold water
    Flour for dredging
    Packaged bread crumbs, for dredging
½ cup vegetable oil
    Lemon wedges (optional)

Pound cutlets as directed; pat dry with paper toweling. If they are large, cut in half. Trim to more or less 3-inch squares. Sprinkle one side of each square with salt and pepper. Trim prosciutto (if using) to squares slightly smaller than the cutlet. Lay a piece of prosciutto on half of the cutlet. Top with slice of mozzarella and cover with remaining turkey squares. Gently press flat with the palm of your hand. Dredge each "sandwich" with flour. Dip into beaten egg, letting excess drip off. Dredge with bread crumbs. Fry slowly in a large skillet in oil combined with butter. When first side is golden brown, turn and brown second side. Total frying time should be about 10 minutes, or until outsides of sandwich are crisp, golden brown and the cheese has melted. Drain on paper toweling and serve with lemon wedges.

Pojarsky Cutlets

The secret is with the nutmeg and cream

Makes 4 servings.

2 pounds (about 4 cups) white and dark meat
    of turkey, well-trimmed
1½ cups crumbled, slightly stale white bread,
    without crusts
¾ cup milk
1 large egg
⅔ cup heavy cream
½ cup butter, softened
    Generous pinch of ground nutmeg
1 cup packaged bread crumbs
1 cup butter or margarine

Put the meat twice through the fine blade of the meat grinder. Soak bread in milk until completely soft, or about 10 minutes. Squeeze out excess milk. Combine turkey, soaked bread, egg, cream, softened butter, salt, pepper and nutmeg and beat with a wooden spoon until smooth, thick and well mixed. Shape into 8 oval patties and dredge with bread crumbs, gently flattening each patty to 1-inch thickness as you do so. Fry slowly in hot butter or margarine until crisp and golden brown on both sides—about 10 minutes in all. Serve with buttered rice or crisply fried shoestring potatoes, and peas or a green salad.

Turkey and Liver Croquettes

Use either fresh meat or left-overs for this delicious treat

Makes 6 servings.

1 pound (about 2 cups) cut up white meat of turkey
¾ pound turkey and/or chicken livers
1 medium size onion, quartered
2 eggs
1½ teaspoons salt
½ teaspoon white pepper
¼ to ½ cup matzoh or cracker meal
Rendered turkey or chicken fat, margarine or butter for frying

1 Only white meat of turkey should be used for this. Put it through the fine blade of the grinder along with livers that were trimmed of all fat and connective tissue, and onion. Add eggs, salt and pepper and beat well with a wooden spoon. Add matzoh or cracker meal, a little at a time until mixture is not too liquid and can be molded, but is still soft and slightly sticky.
2 Melt ½-inch depth of fat in a skillet and when moderately hot, drop ground meat mixture from two wet tablespoons, into hot fat, forming patties about 2 to 2½ inches in diameter and ½ to ¾-inch thick. If you prefer, you can mold these cakes with palms of your hands, but wet them first in cold water so the meat will not stick.
3 Fry slowly until golden brown on one side; turn and fry the second side. Test one croquette to see if it cooked thoroughly and is no longer pink on the inside. Fry the others accordingly. Drain on paper toweling and serve hot. For extra crispness, the uncooked croquettes can be dredged in additional matzoh or cracker meal crumbs.

Turkey Gumbo

A hearty and tasty dish adapted from Louisiana Creole cookery

Makes 12 servings.

1 uncooked turkey carcass with plenty of meat—wings and legs can also be used
2½ to 3 quarts turkey stock
2 tablespoons butter or margarine
2 tablespoons minced raw bacon
1 clove garlic, minced
1 large onion, chopped

1 green pepper, seeded and chopped
1 cup tomato juice or leftover liquid from canned tomatoes or 3 canned tomatoes, chopped, with their liquid
1 teaspoon leaf thyme
1 large bay leaf
Pinch of cayenne, optional and to taste
5 tablespoons butter or rendered bacon fat, or combination
5 tablespoons flour
1 tablespoon filé powder
Steamed white rice

1 Cook turkey with skin and bones if they are on the pieces, as described above for poached turkey. When done, remove meat from bones and reserve; discard bones. Strain and skim stock and return turkey to it.
2 Heat butter and bacon and sauté chopped garlic, onion and pepper until golden brown. Add to soup along with tomato juice, thyme, bay leaf and cayenne. Simmer gently for 30 minutes, adjusting seasoning to taste as you do so.
3 Heat 5 tablespoons of butter in a small heavy bottom saucepan. When bubbling, add flour and stir smooth. Cook very slowly, stirring almost constantly for about 10 minutes, or until roux is a dark coffee color. The flour will seem to take a long time before it begins to color, but once it does, it burns quickly so give it your undivided attention. When a good dark espresso color (but not burned), cool slightly, then stir into the simmering soup.
4 Cook 30 minutes more then add filé powder; simmer 10 minutes more. Adjust seasoning and serve in a bowl with a mound of white rice heaped in center of each serving.

Turkey and Pork Paté

This paté is a perfect way to use left-over turkey for a special treat

Makes 12 servings.

1 pound cut-up turkey meat, white and dark, well-trimmed
1 pound pork shoulder
¼ pound (about) white and dark turkey meat in ¼-to ½-inch strips
¼ pound (about) lean ham (from whole baked ham, ham steak or ham butt) in strips about ½-inch long and ¼-inch thick
½ cup brandy or Madeira
1 teaspoon salt
¼ teaspoon black pepper

Pinch each of ground thyme and allspice
1 *small clove garlic, crushed*
1 *medium size onion, finely minced*
3 *tablespoons butter*
2 *eggs, well beaten*
2 *teaspoons salt*
¼ *teaspoon black pepper*
1 *teaspoon leaf thyme*
1 *large clove garlic, crushed*
¾ *cup unsalted, natural color pistachio nuts, coarsely chopped*
Flat sheets of fresh pork fatback or blanched salt pork, about ⅛-inch thick, to line terrine
2 *small bay leaves*

1 Grind turkey meat and pork (with its own fat) finely and together. Cut strips of white and dark turkey meat from breast and thighs. Combine with ham strips and marinate in brandy or Madeira along with 1 teaspoon salt, ¼ teaspoon black pepper, thyme, allspice and 1 clove of garlic, crushed in a garlic press. Let stand about 30 minutes.

2 Sauté minced onion in 3 tablespoons butter, very slowly, so onion becomes soft but not at all brown. This will take about 10 minutes. Pour marinade from meat strips into pan, and swirl out juices. Add onions, their butter and all pan juices with marinade to turkey and pork mixture and beat together with a wooden spoon. As you do so, add beaten eggs, 2 teaspoons salt, another ¼ teaspoon pepper, thyme, the second clove of garlic, crushed in a press, and the pistachio nuts.

3 Using an 8-cup pâté terrine or casserole that has a tight fitting lid, line the bottom and sides with the thin sheets of pork fat, reserving some for the top of the filled terrine. Place one-third of the ground meat mixture in a layer on the bottom of the casserole. Divide the meat strips in half and arrange alternately on top of the ground meat. Add another third of the ground meat in a layer and on that arrange, alternately, the remaining meat strips. Top with remaining ground meat, patting it evenly into place. Place bay leaves on the meat and cover with remaining sheets of pork fat. Cover that with a sheet of aluminum foil and cover with lid. Place in deep baking pan and pour in boiling water to come halfway up the sides of the terrine.

4 Bake in 350 degree oven for about 1½ hours,
(continued)

The pistachio-studded **Turkey and Pork Paté** makes use of every scrap of meat left on the carcass.

or until pâté shrinks from the sides of the terrine and the juices run clear, with no pink tint.

5 Remove terrine from water bath and set in a pan or on a deep platter. Remove its lid and weight the pâté down by setting a plate, another terrine or a small plank on top of the foil covering the pâté. Be sure this fits inside the rim of the terrine so it presses directly on the pâté. Put something heavy on top of this . . . filled cans, or an old small flat iron, so it will press down and eliminate excess liquid and air spaces.

6 Cool at room temperature then chill, still weighted, for 24 hours before serving so flavor ripens. Serve in slices, directly from the terrine. Makes about 2½ pounds of pâté.

Quenelles of Turkey, Au Gratin

This is gourmet fare that every cook can make—if you follow the directions faithfully

Makes 4 servings.

> 1 pound or 2 cups cut up turkey meat, equal amounts of light and dark meat is preferable
> 1 cup water
> 2 teaspoons salt
> 4 tablespoons unsalted butter
> 1 cup sifted flour
> 3 eggs
> ½ teaspoon ground nutmeg
> ½ teaspoon salt
> ½ teaspoon white pepper
> 2 to 3 tablespoons heavy sweet cream
> 1½ quarts well seasoned turkey stock, or canned chicken broth
> 1 small bay leaf
> 4 tablespoons butter
> 6 tablespoons flour
> 1¼ cups scalded milk
> 1¼ cups hot stock in which quenelles were poached
> ½ cup dry Vermouth or other dry white wine, heated
> ½ teaspoon salt
> Pinch each of mace and cayenne pepper
> ½ cup heavy cream
> Lemon juice, to taste
> Butter
> ¼ cup grated Swiss or Parmesan cheese
> Sweet paprika, for sprinkling

1 Be sure turkey meat is trimmed of all skin, membrane and gristle. Cut in small pieces and put twice through the fine blade of a meat grinder.

2 Bring water to boiling with salt; add butter and when it has melted, remove from heat and stir in, all at once, the cup of flour. Return to low heat and beat until mixture forms a ball and leaves the sides of the pan.

3 Take off the heat and beat in the eggs, one at a time, being sure one is completely incorporated before adding the next. Cool slightly in a mixing bowl and then combine with ground turkey, nutmeg, salt and white pepper. Beat very well with a wooden spoon or in your electric mixer using a pastry blender or in an electric food mill or in a mortar and pestle. The mixture should be worked to a very smooth, sticky paste. Chill for at least an hour, or until you are ready to cook.

4 Before cooking, beat in 3 tablespoons of heavy cream, one spoonful at a time, until mixture is slightly softer but still stiff enough to be shaped.

5 Using two tablespoons dipped in cold water, or your hands, also dipped in cold water, shape 16 quenelles in ovals or as sausages, approximately 3 inches long and 1 inch in diameter, or at the widest point.

6 Pour enough stock into a large skillet to make a 2-inch depth; add bay leaf and bring to boiling. Use two skillets if you have them. Add quenelles in a single layer and lower heat to a simmer. Poach gently for 15 to 20 minutes. Test one quenelle to see if it is firm, opaque and that its juices run clear. When all are done, drain on paper towel and keep warm.

To make sauce, melt 4 tablespoons butter in a saucepan and when bubbling, stir in 6 tablespoons flour. Cook for 2 or 3 minutes, then pour in, all at once, the hot scalded milk, the hot stock and the wine. Beat, preferably with a wire whisk, and cook slowly until smooth and very thick. Season with salt, mace and cayenne. Stir in heavy cream until sauce is a little thinner, but still thick enough to coat a spoon. Adjust seasonings, adding a little lemon juice, or more wine, to taste. Quenelles can be baked in a large single, 2-inch deep open baking dish, or in individual gratins. Butter either, then add a light coating of the cream sauce to the bottom of the baking dish. Arrange quenelles in a single layer, then cover with remaining sauce. Sprinkle with cheese and paprika, and dot with butter. Place under a moderately hot broiler for about 10 minutes, or until top is brown and sauce is bubbling.

HOW TO POACH TURKEY

Cut turkey in quarters, then cut off wings and drumsticks at the joints. If pieces are too large to fit in a stock or soup pot, cut again, right through the bones. The idea is to have the largest possible pieces that will fit into a pot and be covered with a minimum of water. For that, you will need a tall straight-sided pot, usually known as a stock pot or a marmite. Cover turkey and all giblets except liver with cold water . . . three quarts should be enough to cover a 12 pound turkey, and four quarts should cover a 20 pounder. Bring to a boil, uncovered, reduce to a simmer and skim off foam as it rises to the surface. Cover pot and cook slowly but steadily for 1 hour. At that point, add 1 tablespoon salt, 2 stalks of celery with leaves, 2 scraped whole carrots and a large peeled onion. A cleaned leek, a piece of knob celery and a few sprigs of parsley can also be added. Cook for another hour or two until meat is tender and beginning to loosen from bone. Remove turkey, strain broth and remove fat from top, a feat more easily accomplished when the broth is chilled. The broth can be used either as soup or stock for gravy and sauces.

If you use most of the turkey meat raw for other recipes and are left with an uncooked carcass, break it up and cook as above, adding less water as needed, to cover. Usually there will be enough meat on it to make a good soup. If you are left with the carcass but have no definite plans for a soup, cook it in plain water, with a little salt, but do not add any vegetables. Cooked plain, the stock keeps better and is more versatile, as it can be flavored with vegetables when reheated and will taste fresher and be more suitable to whatever you decide to make. Stock will keep 2 or 3 months in the freezer and at least a week in the refrigerator, after which it can be boiled for 5 minutes and rechilled.

Moroccan Couscous

When the company will be large, take the time to prepare this exquisite North African dish

Makes 16 servings.

2 pounds couscous (coarse semolina)
6 cups boiling water, well salted

8 to 10 pound turkey, cut in small stew-size pieces
6 large onions, coarsely chopped
½ cup butter
½ cup olive or vegetable oil
1 tablespoon salt
1 teaspoon black pepper
½ teaspoon ground turmeric
¼ teaspoon cayenne pepper (optional)
1 teaspoon saffron threads, crushed
1 three-inch piece stick cinnamon
5 tomatoes, fresh or canned, peeled, seeded and chopped (5 cups)
Water
6 carrots, scraped and cut in 1½ inch chunks
1 pound zucchini, cut in 1½ inch lengths
3 or 4 turnips, cut in quarters (optional)
1 large or 2 small acorn squash, peeled, seeded and cut in 1½ to 2 inch chunks
3 cups cooked chick peas, rinsed and drained if canned
1 cup black seedless raisins, soaked in liquid from stew
Harissa (Red Pepper Sauce)
⅓ cup crushed, dried Italian hot chili peppers
2 cloves garlic, peeled
2 teaspoons caraway seeds
1 teaspoon fennel seeds (optional)
Pinch of ground cumin (optional)
½ teaspoon salt
3 tablespoons olive oil, or as needed
1½ cups liquid from stew
Juice of ½ lemon
1 tablespoon minced fresh parsley
1 tablespoon minced fresh green coriander, if available

1 If you have a couscous pot, prepare semolina by placing it in a large bowl and pouring over it 2 cups of the boiling salt water. Let stand 20 minutes, fluffing grain occasionally with a fork. Repeat, adding water and fluffing, twice at 20 minute intervals.
2 Line the top of the couscous pot with a double thickness of clean cheesecloth and set aside. If you do not have a couscous pot, cook semolina while stew cooks, following instructions on package for boiling, in water or broth from stew.
3 Cut turkey in stew size chunks, including bones in wing, leg and thigh pieces, but cut thick breast meat in boneless chunks.
4 Place turkey and chopped onions, with butter and vegetable oil in the bottom of the couscous pot, or in a large (8 quart) soup pot. Add salt, pepper, turmeric, cayenne, saffron and cinnamon.
5 Cook gently, covered, for 20 minutes, swirling pan and stirring occasionally until meat and

(continued)

onion take on a golden color and look slightly braised. Add enough water to come just to the level of the meat. Cover and simmer for 1½ to 2 hours, or until meat is tender. This much of the stew can be prepared in advance. Skim off excess fat.

6 Half an hour before serving, add tomatoes, carrots, zucchini and turnips and simmer until tender.

7 At the same time, place the couscous grain over the bottom part of the steamer and seal rim of bottom pot to the top by wrapping it in aluminum foil. Cover top and let grain steam as vegetables cook, fluffing grain by tossing it with a fork two or three times during the process. Add acorn squash and chick peas to stew and cook until tender.

To prepare Harissa Sauce: Grind chili peppers, garlic, caraway, fennel seeds, cumin and salt, in a mortar and pestle or in a spice mill. Stir in 1 teaspoon olive oil. This can be done in advance and kept in the refrigerator. Just before serving, stir 2 teaspoons of this mixture into 1½ cups of broth from stew, adding 2 tablespoons olive oil and lemon juice. Adjust seasonings, adding salt if needed. Stir in chopped parsley and/or coriander. Serve in small sauce bowl, to be spooned over couscous.

To serve Couscous: Portion couscous into large individual bowls (old-fashioned soup plates would be perfect), make a well in the center and in it put meat, vegetables and broth. Top with raisins.

Although lamb is more common in colorful, savory, one-pot **Moroccan Couscous,** turkey is also traditional and just as good.

POPULAR TURKEY STUFFINGS

Double Rice Stuffing

Makes about 10 cups, or enough to stuff a 12-pound turkey

    2 packages (6 ounces each) long-grain and
        wild-rice mix
    6 tablespoons (¾ stick) butter or margarine
 4½ cups water
    3 cups chopped celery
    1 large onion, chopped (1 cup)
    1 jar (7 ounces) pimiento-stuffed olives,
        drained and sliced
    1 teaspoon salt
    ¼ teaspoon pepper

1 Prepare rice mix with 2 tablespoons of the butter or margarine and the 4½ cups water, following label directions.
2 Sauté celery and onion in remaining butter or margarine until soft in a large frying pan; lightly stir in rice mixture, olives, salt, and pepper.

Brown Rice Stuffing

Makes about 10 cups, or enough to stuff a 12-pound turkey

    9 cups water
    1 tablespoon salt
    3 cups brown rice (1½ boxes, 12 ounces each)
    2 cups chopped celery
    1 medium-size onion, grated
    ½ cup (1 stick) butter or margarine
    ½ cup chopped parsley
    2 teaspoons salt
 1½ teaspoons poultry seasoning

1 Combine water and the 1 tablespoon salt in a kettle. Heat to boiling. Stir in rice; reduce heat; cover. Simmer 45 minutes, or until rice is tender. Drain; place in a large bowl.
2 Sauté celery and onion in butter or margarine until soft in a medium-size skillet. Stir in parsley, the remaining 2 teaspoons salt, and poultry seasoning.
3 Pour over rice; stir lightly until evenly mixed.

Celery, poultry seasoning, pepper, parsley, and white bread are the heroes in **Herb Stuffing.**

Sausage and Apple Stuffing

Makes about 10 cups, or enough to stuff a 12-pound turkey

    8 cups cubed white bread (16 slices)
    1 pound sausage meat
    1 large onion, chopped (1 cup)
    2 large apples, pared, quartered, cored, and
       chopped
    ½ cup water
    1 teaspoon salt

1 Spread bread cubes on large cooky sheets; place in very slow oven (250°) 10 minutes; remove from oven; reserve.
2 Cut sausage into 8 thick slices. Brown 5 minutes on each side in a medium-size skillet, then break into small pieces. Cook 1 minute longer, or until no trace of pink remains. Combine with bread cubes in a large bowl.
3 Pour off drippings from skillet; measure; return 2 tablespoons. Add onions and sauté until tender. Stir in water and apples; heat to boiling. Pour over sausage mixture; add salt; toss lightly until evenly moist.

Herb Stuffing

Makes about 10 cups, or enough to stuff a 12-pound turkey

    1 large onion, chopped (1 cup)
    1 cup (2 sticks) butter or margarine
    1 cup finely chopped celery
    2 envelopes instant chicken broth or 2 tea-
       spoons granulated chicken bouillon
    1 teaspoon poultry seasoning
    ½ teaspoon salt
    ¼ teaspoon seasoned pepper
    1¼ cups water
    12 cups cubed white bread (24 slices)
    ¾ cup chopped parsley

1 Sauté onion in butter or margarine until soft in a medium-size frying pan; stir in celery, chicken broth, poultry seasoning, salt, pepper, and water; heat to boiling.
2 Pour over bread and parsley in a large bowl; toss lightly until evenly moist.

German Potato Stuffing

Makes about 12 cups, or enough to stuff a 12-
to 14-pound turkey

½ cup shortening
8 tablespoons (1 stick) butter or margarine
16 large potatoes, pared and diced (about 16
cups)
3 large onions, chopped (3 cups)
1 cup thinly sliced celery
4 teaspoons salt
½ teaspoon pepper
½ cup milk
3 cups coarse slightly dry white-bread crumbs
(6 slices)
4 eggs
6 tablespoons chopped parsley

1 Melt shortening and butter or margarine in
a large frying pan.
2 Stir in potatoes, onions, celery, salt, and pepper; cover loosely.
3 Cook slowly, stirring often, 30 minutes, or
until potatoes are tender.
4 Pour milk over bread crumbs in a small bowl;
stir into potato mixture, then stir in eggs. Con-

tinue cooking, stirring constantly, until eggs are
cooked. (Flecks of cooked egg will show in the
stuffing.) Remove from heat.
5 Stir in parsley. Cool slightly.

Dixie Belle Stuffing

Makes about 10 cups, or enough to stuff a
12-pound turkey

1 pound sausage meat
2 packages (8 ounces each) ready-mix
corn-bread stuffing
2 large onions, diced (2 cups)
2 cups diced celery
1¼ cups water
½ cup chopped parsley

1 Cut sausage in 8 thick slices. Brown 5 minutes
on each side in a medium-size frying pan, then
break in small chunks. Cook 1 minute longer,
or until no pink remains. Remove with a slotted
spoon and combine with stuffing mix in a large
bowl.
2 Stir onions and celery into drippings in pan;

When you cook two turkeys at one time, don't just double the amount of stuffing.
Be creative—make two different stuffings.

When your favorite stuffing recipe doesn't fill the huge bird at hand, don't let that put you off. Just multiply the recipe. Any excess can be served up with the left-overs, for a secondary treat.

sauté until soft. Stir in water; heat to boiling. Pour over sausage mixture; add parsley; toss lightly until evenly moist.

Mushroom Stuffing

Makes about 10 cups, or enough to stuff a 12-pound turkey

    1 pound fresh mushrooms
  10 bunches green onions
    1 cup (2 sticks) butter or margarine
  12 cups coarse soft white-bread crumbs (24 slices)
    1 teaspoon salt

1 Wash mushrooms and trim; chop caps and stems. (There will be about 5½ cups.)
2 Trim onions and slice. (There will be about 6 cups.)

3 Sauté mushrooms and onions in butter or margarine in a large frying pan 10 minutes, or just until wilted. Pour over bread crumbs in a large bowl; sprinkle with salt; toss lightly until evenly moist.

Peanut Stuffing

Makes about 10 cups, or enough to stuff a 12-pound turkey

    1 medium-size onion, chopped (½ cup)
    2 cups chopped celery
  ¾ cup (1½ sticks) butter or margarine
  2½ cups water
    2 packages (7 ounces each) seasoned stuffing croutons
    1 cup salted peanuts, ground fine

(continued)

1 Sauté onion and celery in butter or margarine until soft in a large frying pan. Stir in water; heat to boiling.
2 Pour over croutons and peanuts in a large bowl; toss until evenly moist.

Sausage Stuffing

Makes about 6 cups, or enough to stuff an 8-pound turkey

½ pound sausage meat
4 cups cubed slightly dry white bread (8 slices)
2 tablespoons milk
1 cup diced celery
½ teaspoon salt
½ teaspoon poultry seasoning
⅛ teaspoon pepper

1 Brown sausage slowly in a small frying pan, breaking meat up with a fork as it cooks; remove with a slotted spoon and place in a medium-size bowl. Add bread cubes; drizzle with milk.
2 Stir celery into drippings in pan; sauté until soft; stir in salt, poultry seasoning, and pepper.
3 Pour over bread mixture; toss until evenly moist.

Raisin-Walnut Stuffing

Makes 10 cups, or enough to stuff a 12-pound turkey

2 cups seedless raisins
1½ cups water
2 cups chopped celery
1 large onion, chopped (1 cup)
½ cup (1 stick) butter or margarine
1 envelope instant chicken broth or 1 teaspoon granulated chicken bouillon
1 teaspoon salt
1 teaspoon powdered sage
¼ teaspoon pepper
8 cups cubed white bread (16 slices)
2 cups coarsely chopped walnuts

1 Simmer raisins in water in a small saucepan for 1 minute; reserve.
2 Sauté celery and onion in butter or margarine until soft in a large skillet. Stir in chicken broth, salt, sage, and pepper.
3 Add to bread cubes and walnuts in a large bowl; add raisin-water mixture; toss lightly until evenly moist.

Parsley-Egg Stuffing

Makes about 12 cups, or enough to stuff a 12- to 14-pound turkey

1 large onion, chopped (1 cup)
½ cup (1 stick) butter or margarine
1 envelope instant chicken broth
OR: 1 chicken bouillon cube
1½ teaspoons salt
1 cup water
10 cups cubed slightly dry white bread (about 20 slices)
3 hard-cooked eggs, shelled and chopped
½ cup chopped parsley

1 Sauté onion in butter or margarine until soft in a small frying pan; stir in chicken broth or bouillon cube, salt, and water. Heat to boiling, crushing bouillon cube, if used, with spoon.
2 Pour over bread cubes in a large bowl; toss lightly until evenly moist. Fold in eggs and parsley.

Southwest Corn Bread Stuffing

Makes about 6 cups, or enough to stuff the neck cavity of a 12-pound turkey

1 cup chopped celery
1 large onion chopped, (1 cup)
½ cup (1 stick) butter or margarine
1 teaspoon chili powder
1 package (8 ounces) ready-mix corn bread stuffing
¼ cup chopped pimiento-stuffed olives
1 egg
⅓ cup water

1 Sauté celery and onion in butter or margarine until soft in a large skillet. Stir in chili powder; cook 1 minute longer. Remove from heat; stir in stuffing mix and olives.
2 Beat egg slightly with water in a small bowl; pour over stuffing mixture in skillet; toss lightly until evenly moist.

Chestnut-Celery Stuffing

Makes 3 cups, or enough to stuff the neck cavity of a 6-pound turkey

¾ pound fresh chestnuts
1 cup cubed white bread (2 slices)

½ cup diced celery
1 small onion, chopped (¼ cup)
2 tablespoons butter or margarine
1 can (3 or 4 ounces) chopped mushrooms
¾ teaspoon salt
⅛ teaspoon pepper
½ teaspoon poultry seasoning

1 Wash chestnuts; cut slits in each shell; place in a shallow baking pan. Bake in very hot oven (475°) 15 minutes. Remove chestnuts; lower oven temperature to very slow (250°). When cool enough to handle, shell and skin nuts.
2 Cook, covered, in boiling salted water to cover, in a medium-size saucepan, about 15 minutes, or until tender; drain; chop fine. (You should have about 1½ cups.)
3 While chestnuts are cooking, spread bread cubes on a large cooky sheet; place in very slow (250°) oven 10 minutes; remove from oven; reserve.
4 Sauté celery and onion in butter or margarine just until soft in a medium-size skillet. Combine with chestnuts in a medium-size bowl.
5 Add mushrooms and their liquid, salt, pepper, bread cubes, and poultry seasoning; toss lightly until evenly moist.

Vegetable Stuffing

Makes about 6 cups, or enough to stuff an 8-pound turkey

1 large onion, chopped (1 cup)
4 tablespoons (½ stick) butter or margarine
¼ cup chopped parsley
2 tablespoons chopped stuffed green olives
6 water chestnuts (from a 5-ounce can), chopped
¼ cup hot water
4 cups herb-seasoned stuffing croutons (from a 7-ounce package)

1 Sauté onion in butter or margarine until soft in a small frying pan; stir in parsley, olives, water chestnuts, and water.
2 Pour over croutons in a medium-size bowl; toss until evenly moist.

Apple Stuffing

Makes about 4 cups, or enough to stuff a 6-pound turkey

1 large apple, pared, quartered, cored, and chopped

1 medium-size onion, chopped (½ cup)
2 tablespoons butter or margarine
1 envelope instant chicken broth or 1 teaspoon granulated chicken bouillon
¼ cup water
½ teaspoon leaf rosemary, crumbled
5 cups toasted bread cubes

1 Sauté apple and onion in butter or margarine until soft in a small frying pan.
2 Stir in chicken broth, water, and rosemary; heat to boiling. Pour over bread cubes in a large bowl; toss lightly until evenly moist.

LEFT-OVER TURKEY

Turkey Hawaiian

Pineapple, almonds and crisp vegetables turn cooked turkey into this showy tempter

Makes 6 servings

1 large onion, chopped (1 cup)
2 tablespoons vegetable oil
1 package (10 ounces) frozen peas
1½ cups sliced celery
2 envelopes instant chicken broth
  OR: 2 chicken-bouillon cubes
¾ cup water
2 tablespoons cornstarch
1 tablespoon soy sauce
2 cans (8¾ ounces each) pineapple chunks
1 can (3 or 4 ounces) sliced mushrooms
1 can (5 ounces) water chestnuts, drained and sliced
½ cup whole blanched almonds
3 cups julienne strips of cooked turkey
  Fluffy hot rice

1 Sauté onion in vegetable oil just until soft in large frying pan.
2 Stir in frozen peas, celery, instant chicken broth or bouillon cubes and water. Cover; heat to boiling; simmer 5 minutes.
3 Blend cornstarch and soy sauce until smooth in 2-cup measure. Drain and stir in syrup from pineapple and liquid from mushrooms. Stir into vegetable mixture. Cook, stirring often, until sauce thickens and boils 3 minutes.
4 Stir in pineapple, mushrooms, water chestnuts, almonds and 2 cups of turkey. (Save re-

(continued)

maining 1 cup for topping.) Cover; heat slowly until hot.

5 Spoon hot rice in a ring on heated serving plates; mound turkey mixture in center; top with saved turkey strips, arranged crisscross fashion. Garnish with sliced kumquat and crystallized ginger.

Turkey Stroganoff

Heat cooked turkey in a no-fuss creamy sauce for this quickie with a Continental flavor

Makes 4 to 6 servings

1 large onion, chopped (1 cup)
2 tablespoons butter or margarine
2 to 3 cups julienne strips of cooked turkey
1½ cups turkey gravy
    OR: 1 can (10½ ounces) chicken gravy
2 tablespoons catsup
1 cup dairy sour cream
    Parsley noodles

1 Sauté onion in butter or margarine just until soft in large frying pan. Stir in turkey, turkey or chicken gravy and catsup; simmer 5 minutes.
2 Stir in sour cream; heat *just to boiling.* Serve over hot noodles tossed with chopped parsley.

Skillet Turkey Scramble

Turkey and ham go with rice, tomatoes and seasonings in this top-of-the-range winner

Makes 6 servings

1 medium-size onion, chopped (½ cup)
1 clove of garlic, minced
2 tablespoons butter or margarine
1 teaspoon salt
½ teaspoon chili powder
⅛ teaspoon pepper
    Dash of cayenne
1 bay leaf
2 cans (1 pound each) stewed tomatoes
2 cups diced cooked turkey
1 can (8 ounces) chopped ham sticks, diced
    OR: 2 cups diced cooked ham
1 cup uncooked regular rice
1 tablespoon chopped parsley

1 Sauté onion and garlic in butter or margarine just until soft in large frying pan. Stir in seasonings, then remaining ingredients; cover.

2 Simmer, stirring often, 40 minutes, or until rice is tender and liquid is absorbed. Remove bay leaf.

Tureen Turkey Treat

Hearty with vegetables and meat, it's a most inviting warmer-upper on a brisk day

Makes 6 generous servings

SAVORY TURKEY BROTH *(recipe follows)*
¼ pound salt pork, diced
1 large onion, chopped (1 cup)
3 cups diced raw potatoes
1 cup diced celery
½ teaspoon salt
⅛ teaspoon pepper
1 can (about 1 pound) cream-style corn
1 large can (14½ ounces) evaporated milk
1½ cups diced cooked turkey
½ teaspoon leaf marjoram, crumbled
½ teaspoon leaf thyme, crumbled

1 Make SAVORY TURKEY BROTH and set aside for Step 3.
2 Sauté salt pork until crisp in kettle; push to one side. Add onion; sauté just until soft.
3 Stir in potatoes, celery, salt, pepper and saved broth; cover; simmer 20 minutes, or until potatoes are tender.
4 Stir in corn, evaporated milk, turkey and seasonings. Heat just to boiling. Ladle into heated soup bowls or plates.
    SAVORY TURKEY BROTH—Break turkey carcass to fit into a kettle. Add 1 sliced onion, 1 sliced carrot, handful of celery tops, 1 tablespoon salt, ¼ teaspoon pepper and 6 cups water; cover. Heat to boiling, then simmer 1 hour. Lift out carcass and, when cool enough to handle, remove and dice any bits of meat. Place in small bowl; cover and chill until ready to make soup. Strain broth into medium-size bowl; then chill enough to skim fat from top. Add water, if needed, to make 6 cups.

Turkey Puffs

Golden popovers are halved and filled with turkey salad lightly seasoned with curry

Bake popovers at 400° for 50 minutes.
Makes 6 sandwiches

3 eggs
1 cup milk
1 cup sifted all-purpose flour

½ teaspoon salt
6 slices bacon
6 leaves Boston lettuce
   CURRIED TURKEY SALAD *(recipe follows)*

1 Beat eggs just until foamy in a medium-size bowl; add milk, flour and salt all at once; beat briskly ½ minute. Scrape down side of bowl; beat 1½ minutes longer. (Batter will be thin and smooth.)
2 Pour into 6 well-greased 6-ounce custard cups, filling each ⅔ full. Set cups, not touching, in a shallow pan.
3 Bake in hot oven (400°) 50 minutes, or until puffed and golden-brown; remove from cups. Poke a small hole in side of each to let steam escape; cool on a wire rack.
4 Sauté bacon until almost crisp in a large frying pan; roll each slice around the tines of a fork to make a curl; drain on paper toweling.
5 Cut popovers in half lengthwise; line half of each with lettuce, then fill with CURRIED TURKEY SALAD, dividing evenly. Garnish with bacon curls and serve with remaining popover halves.

Curried Turkey Salad

Go easy on the curry powder, and you'll discover a new way to use up left-over turkey

Makes about 6 cups

  4 cups cubed cooked turkey
  2 tablespoons minced onion
  2 cups chopped celery
1¼ cups mayonnaise or salad dressing
  1 teaspoon curry powder
  1 teaspoon sugar
  1 teaspoon salt
  2 teaspoons lemon juice
  2 teaspoons grated onion

1 Combine turkey, minced onion and celery in a large bowl.
2 Blend mayonnaise or salad dressing, curry powder, sugar, salt, lemon juice and grated onion in a small bowl; spoon over turkey; toss to mix well. Chill.

Light as a feather, but filled with a punch that everyone will enjoy, **Turkey Puffs** are easy to make.

Springtime is anytime you dress up Cornish Hens for a **Springtime Party Platter.** *(See recipe p. 75.)*

Duck, Cornish Hen, and Goose

Traditionally, these are not the usual festival birds. But they could be if you tried them out. Each one has a distinctive taste that would appeal—if given half the chance—and in the following pages there are plenty of recipes to select from.

Twin Duck Barbecue

Use kitchen shears to cut each tender duck into serving-size quarters

Makes 8 servings

2 frozen ready-to-cook ducklings (about 4½ pounds each), thawed
6 cups water
  Handfull of celery tops
1 small onion, sliced
4 peppercorns
  Orange-spice Barbecue Sauce (recipe follows)

1 Pierce skin of ducklings all over with fork so fat will cook out.
2 Simmer, covered, in water with celery tops, onion, and peppercorns in large kettle 2 hours, or just until barely tender. Remove ducks and drain well. (This much can be done ahead.)
3 When ready to grill, place ducks on grill about 10 inches above hot coals; brush with *Orange-Spice Barbecue Sauce*. Grill, turning and basting often, 1½ hours, or until joints move easily and ducks are a rich golden brown.
4 Cut each into quarters for serving.

Orange-Spice Barbecue Sauce

It gives a golden-glaze goodness to grilled ducklings. Delicious with chicken, too

Makes 1½ cups

¼ cup sugar
2 tablespoons cornstarch
½ teaspoon ground allspice
½ teaspoon ground cloves
1 cup orange juice
2 tablespoons vinegar
4 tablespoons (½ stick) butter or margarine

Combine sugar, cornstarch, allspice, and cloves in small saucepan; stir in orange juice and vinegar. Cook, stirring constantly, until sauce thickens and boils 3 minutes. Stir in butter or margarine.

Roast Duckling Jubilee

Three birds glazed sparkly-brown and arranged atop gourmetlike rice make a showy platter

Roast at 325° for 3 hours.
Makes 12 servings

3 ready-to-cook ducklings (about 4 pounds each)
1 teaspoon salt
3 small onions, peeled and quartered
1 medium-size apple, quartered, cored, and cubed
1 can (1 pound) whole figs
1 can (1 pound) dark sweet cherries
1 can (6 ounces) frozen concentrated orange juice, thawed
  Pecan Pilaf (recipe follows)
3 preserved kumquats
  Jubilee Sauce (recipe follows)

1 Wash ducklings inside and out with cold water; dry well. Pierce skin all over with a fork so fat will cook out.
2 Sprinkle cavity of each bird with part of the salt; stuff with onion quarters and apple cubes. Place ducklings, side by side, on a rack in a large roasting pan. (Or use two smaller pans, if necessary.)
3 Roast, uncovered, in slow oven (325°) 2½ hours.
4 While ducklings cook, drain syrups from figs and cherries into separate cups. Measure out ¼ cup of the fig syrup and 2 tablespoons of

(continued)

the cherry syrup and mix with ¼ cup of the concentrated orange juice in a small bowl. (Set fruits and remaining syrups and orange juice aside for garnish in Step 7 and *Jubilee Sauce*.)
5 Brush ducklings with part of the orange mixture. Continue roasting, brushing several times with more orange mixture, 30 minutes, or until a drumstick joint moves easily and ducklings are richly golden. (During roasting, pierce skin several times with a fork and, to keep fat from smoking, remove from pan with a baster or dip out with a spoon.)
6 Spoon *Pecan Pilaf* onto a heated large serving platter; arrange ducklings on top.
7 Thread 3 figs and 2 cherries, alternately, onto each of 3 long kebab sticks; top each with a preserved kumquat; place around ducklings on platter.
8 Carve ducklings into quarters or cut with kitchen scissors; serve with *Jubilee Sauce*.

JUBILEE SAUCE—Mix 2 tablespoons cornstarch, ½ teaspoon salt, ¼ teaspoon dry mustard, and a dash of allspice in a medium-size saucepan. Blend in 1 cup water, ½ cup of the remaining concentrated orange juice, and ½ cup of the fig syrup. Cook, stirring constantly, until sauce thickens and boils 3 minutes. Stir in 2 tablespoons butter or margarine until melted, then remaining cherries and 2 teaspoons Worcestershire sauce; heat just until bubbly. Makes about 3 cups.
Hostess Note—Sauce may be made several hours ahead and reheated slowly until bubbly hot just before serving.

Roast Duckling

It's smart planning to buy an extra bird just to have on hand to turn into a delectable second-day treat

Roast at 325° about 3 hours.
Makes enough for 2 meals, 6 servings each

3 *frozen ready-to-cook ducklings (about 4½*
    pounds each), thawed
2 *teaspoons salt*
¼ *teaspoon pepper*
3 *small onions, peeled and quartered*
    Duck Giblet Broth (recipe follows)
    Golden Gravy (recipe follows)
    Pumpernickel Stuffing (recipe follows)

1 Wash and dry ducklings. Pierce skin all over with fork so fat will cook out. (Set giblets aside to simmer for broth.)
2 Rub skin with mixture of salt and pepper; stuff

4 onion quarters into cavity of each bird; place on rack in large roasting pan. (Or use two small pans, if necessary.)
3 Roast, uncovered, in slow oven (325°) 3 hours, or until drumstick joints move easily and ducklings are a rich golden-brown. (During roasting, pierce skin with fork several times. Also, to keep fat from smoking, dip it from roasting pan into a bowl several times during cooking. There will be as much as 6 cupfuls.)
4 Cut 2 ducklings into quarters. (Poultry shears do a fast job.) Arrange on heated serving platter. Serve with *Golden Gravy* and *Pumpernickel Stuffing*. (Set other duckling aside to cool.)
5 Wrap cooled duckling; chill with 4 cups of *Duck Giblet Broth* for *Duck Pilaf* for another meal.

Duck Giblet Broth

This is making the best use of the whole bird

Makes 6 cups.

Combine giblets (except liver) and necks with 1 medium-size onion, chopped; handful of celery tops; 2 teaspoons salt; and 6 cups water in large saucepan. Simmer 1 hour, or until tender. Add livers for last 20 minutes' cooking. Strain stock; measure; add water, if needed, to make 6 cups. Save 4 cups for making *Duck Pilaf*. Grind or chop giblets fine and add to remaining 2 cups broth for *Golden Gravy*.

Golden Gravy

There's little in the making, but lots in the flavor

Makes about 2½ cups.

Remove rack from roasting pan. Tip pan and pour off all fat into a bowl. Return 4 tablespoons to pan; blend in 4 tablespoons flour; cook, stirring all the time, just until mixture bubbles. Stir in 2 cups broth with ground giblets; continue cooking and stirring, scraping baked-on juices from bottom and sides of pan, until gravy thickens and boils 1 minute. Season to taste with salt and pepper.

Bring a Dickensian flavor to your festival table with **Roast Duckling** and enjoy a taste-treat that is new and exciting.

Pumpernickel Stuffing

Just peppery enough to go with juicy roast duck

Bake at 325° for 1 hour.
Makes 6 servings

3 medium-size onions, chopped (1½ cups)
4 tablespoons drippings from ducklings
3 cups slightly dry pumpernickel-bread cubes
  (6 slices)
3 cups slightly dry white bread cubes (6 slices)
½ cup water
1 teaspoon salt
¼ teaspoon pepper

1 Sauté onions in drippings just until soft in large frying pan. Add bread cubes, water, salt, and pepper; toss lightly to mix. Spoon into 6-cup baking dish.
2 Bake with ducklings in slow oven (325°) 1 hour, or until crisp on top.

Duck Pilaf

Sauté rice first to give it a toasty flavor, then blend with duckling and apricots to make this gourmetlike casserole

Bake at 350° for 1½ hours.
Makes 6 servings

1 roasted duckling
1 cup uncooked regular rice
3 tablespoons vegetable oil
1 cup chopped celery
4 cups broth (from Duck Giblet Broth)
1 teaspoon salt
¼ teaspoon pepper
½ cup cut-up dried apricots

1 Remove skin from duckling; strip meat from frame, then dice. (There should be 3 cups.) Set aside for Step 4.
2 Sauté rice in vegetable oil in large frying pan, stirring often, just until golden; add celery and sauté 5 minutes longer.
3 Stir in broth, salt, and pepper; heat to boiling.
4 Spoon into 8-cup baking dish; stir in duckling and apricots; cover.
5 Bake in moderate oven (350°) 1½ hours, or until rice is tender and liquid is absorbed.

Roast Ducklings Halakahiki

For an even more special treat, cook duck the Brazilian way

Roast at 325° for 2½ hours.
Makes 8 servings

2 ready-to-cook ducklings (about 5 pounds each)
2 teaspoons salt
2 tablespoons lemon juice
9 slices white bread, toasted and cubed
1 cup sliced green onions
2 cloves of garlic, sliced
½ teaspoon ground ginger
2 cans (3 or 4 ounces each) chopped mushrooms, drained
1 can (1 pound, 14 ounces) sliced pineapple
¾ cup (1½ sticks) butter or margarine, melted
¼ cup soy sauce
¼ cup honey
  Mint
  Mandarin Sauce (recipe follows)

1 Wash ducklings inside and out with cold water; dry well. Sprinkle salt and lemon juice into cavities. Smooth neck skin over back, then twist wing tips until they rest flat against sides.
2 Combine bread cubes, green onions, garlic, ginger, and mushrooms in a large bowl.
3 Drain syrup from pineapple into a small bowl and set aside for sauce. Dice 4 slices of the pineapple and add to bread mixture. Drizzle ½ cup of the melted butter or margarine over top; toss lightly to mix.
4 Spoon into cavities in ducklings, packing in

Duckling can make any dinner a special occasion. Try **Roast Ducklings Halakahiki,** given extra appetite appeal by a glistening soy glaze.

lightly. Lace openings together with poultry pins or skewers and string. Place ducklings on a rack in a shallow roasting pan. Do not add any water or cover pan.

5 Roast in slow oven (325°) 1½ hours; pour all drippings from pan.

6 Combine remaining ¼ cup melted butter or margarine with soy sauce and honey in a small saucepan; heat, stirring constantly, to boiling. Brush part over ducklings.

7 Continue roasting, brushing with remaining soy mixture every 15 minutes, 1 hour, or until a drumstick moves easily and ducklings are richly golden.

8 Remove ducklings to a heated large serving platter. Garnish with remaining pineapple slices cut in half and mint.

9 Carve ducklings into quarters or cut with kitchen scissors; serve with *Mandarin Sauce.*

MANDARIN SAUCE—Mix 2 tablespoons cornstarch, ½ teaspoon ground ginger, and 2 envelopes instant chicken broth or 2 teaspoons granulated chicken bouillon in a small saucepan. Drain syrup from 1 can (about 11 ounces) mandarin orange segments into a 2-cup measure; add pineapple syrup and water, if needed, to make 2 cups; stir into cornstarch mixture. Cook, stirring constantly, until sauce thickens and boils 3 minutes; remove from heat. Fold in orange segments. Serve warm. Makes about 2½ cups.

Pecan Pilaf

Cook the rice a day ahead, so each grain will be fluffy-dry and separate before frying.

Makes 12 servings

6 cups water
3 envelopes instant chicken broth·
OR: 3 chicken bouillon cubes
3 cups uncooked regular rice
1 large onion, chopped
½ cup vegetable oil
1½ teaspoons salt
¼ teaspoon mace
1 cup chopped pecans

1 Heat water with chicken broth or bouillon cubes to boiling in a kettle; stir in rice; cover. Cook 20 minutes, or just until rice is tender and liquid is absorbed.

2 Spoon into a large shallow pan; cool, then chill, for rice should be very dry, with each grain separate, before frying. (This should be done a day ahead.)

3 When ready to finish dish, sauté onion in 2 tablespoons of the vegetable oil until soft in a large frying pan; remove with a slotted spoon and place in a kettle. Add 2 more tablespoons of the vegetable oil to frying pan.

4 Fluff rice with a fork to separate grains; stir one third into frying pan. Sauté, stirring gently several times, until lightly golden; remove and place in kettle. Repeat with remaining rice, half at a time, and vegetable oil; return all rice mixture to pan.

(continued p. 73)

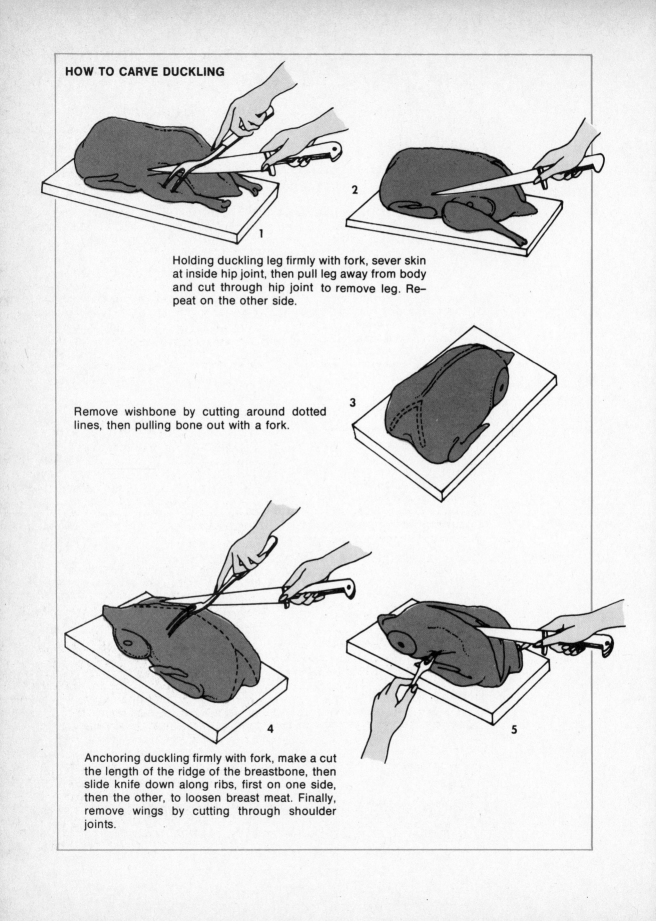

HOW TO CARVE DUCKLING

Holding duckling leg firmly with fork, sever skin at inside hip joint, then pull leg away from body and cut through hip joint to remove leg. Repeat on the other side.

Remove wishbone by cutting around dotted lines, then pulling bone out with a fork.

Anchoring duckling firmly with fork, make a cut the length of the ridge of the breastbone, then slide knife down along ribs, first on one side, then the other, to loosen breast meat. Finally, remove wings by cutting through shoulder joints.

5 Stir in salt, mace, and pecans; cover. Heat slowly 8 minutes, or until hot.
Hostess note—Rice may be sautéed several hours before serving. Cover pan and keep at room temperature. Just before serving, reheat *very slowly*, allowing 15 to 20 minutes.

Roast Duck Orientale

In Chinese fashion the meat steams moist and tender from the inside as it roasts crispy brown outside

Roast at 500° for 30 minutes,
then at 325° for 1 hour.
Makes 4 servings

1 ready-to-cook duckling (about 4 pounds)
2 tablespoons soy sauce
1 tablespoon sugar
1 tablespoon pumpkin-pie spice
1 teaspoon anise seeds
½ teaspoon ground ginger
1 cup boiling water
4 cups shredded romaine

1 Wash duckling inside and out under running cold water; dry well. Skewer neck skin to back of bird; twist wing tips until they rest flat against skewered neck skin.
2 Mix soy sauce, sugar, pumpkin-pie spice, anise seeds, and ginger in a cup. Rub into skin and inside of duckling, then pour any remaining mixture into cavity. Place duck, breast down, on a plate; cover loosely; chill overnight.
3 When ready to roast duckling, mix any sauce on plate with boiling water; pour into body cavity, then close opening tightly with skewers. Place duck, breast up, on a rack in roasting pan. Do not cover pan or add any water.
4 Roast in very hot oven (500°) 30 minutes; lower heat to slow (325°). Remove duckling from oven; dip all fat from pan with a spoon or baster, then return duckling to oven.
5 Continue roasting, spooning off fat as it cooks out, 1 hour, or until tender. (Drumstick should feel soft and twist and move easily.)
6 Place shredded romaine on a heated serving platter. Remove skewers from duckling, then set duckling on platter. Cut in four serving-size pieces with poultry shears, letting juices from cavity flow over romaine. Serve the duckling at once while the skin is at its crispiest, along with the romaine.

Pato De Natal

For an even more special treat, cook duck the Brazilian-way

Roast at 325° for 2½ hours.
Makes 8 servings

2 ready-to-cook ducklings (about 5 pounds each)
1½ cups dry white wine
¼ cup lemon juice
2 teaspoons salt
1 clove of garlic, minced
¼ cup chopped parsley
¼ cup sliced green onions
1 large onion, chopped (1 cup)
4 tablespoons (½ stick) butter or margarine
1 can (1 pound) chestnuts, drained and chopped
¼ teaspoon ground nutmeg
¼ teaspoon pepper
3 cups small slightly dry bread cubes (6 slices)
¼ cup sifted all-purpose flour

1 Remove giblets from cavities of ducklings. Wash ducklings inside and out with cold water; dry well. Place in a large shallow dish. Chop giblets.
2 Mix wine, lemon juice, salt, garlic, parsley, and green onions in a small bowl; pour over ducklings. Let stand, turning several times, at least 4 hours at room temperature, or overnight in refrigerator, to season.
3 Sauté large onion in butter or margarine until soft in a large frying pan; stir in chopped giblets. Cook, stirring several times, 5 minutes. Stir in chestnuts, nutmeg, and pepper. Pour over bread cubes in a large bowl; toss lightly until evenly moist.
4 Remove ducklings from marinade; pat dry. Strain marinade into a 2-cup measure and set aside for making gravy. Stuff chestnut mixture into neck cavities of ducklings; smooth neck skin over back, then twist wing tips until they rest flat against back. Stuff body cavities; lace openings together with poultry pins or skewers and string. Place ducklings, breast up and side by side, on a rack in a large roasting pan. Do not cover pan.
5 Roast in slow oven (325°) 2½ hours, or until ducklings are tender and richly browned. (During roasting, prick skin several times with a fork and, to keep fat from smoking, remove from pan with a baster or dip out with a spoon.) Remove ducklings to a heated large serving platter; keep warm while making gravy.

(continued)

6 Pour all fat from roasting pan into a cup, then measure ¼ cupful and return to pan. Blend in flour; cook, stirring constantly, until bubbly. Add water to marinade to make 2 cups; stir into roasting pan. Continue cooking and stirring until gravy thickens and boils 1 minute.

7 Garnish ducklings with parsley and ruffled green-onion tops threaded through thin lemon slices, if you wish. Carve ducklings; serve gravy separately to spoon over meat and stuffing.

Long Island Duckling Bigarade

Bigarade is a blending of the Quick Brown Sauce and cooked orange peel—for the orange glaze

Roast at 400° for 1 hour and 30 minutes.
Makes 4 servings.

1 frozen duckling (about 5 pounds), thawed
    Salt
¾ cup chopped celery
¾ cup chopped carrot
1 medium-size onion, chopped (½ cup)
2 bay leaves
1 tablespoon all-purpose flour
¼ cup Madeira wine
    QUICK BROWN SAUCE (recipe follows)

You don't have to dine out to enjoy **Long Island Duck Bigarade.** Bring the dine-out atmosphere into your home with good company and this gourmet dish.

½ cup currant jelly
1 cup sugar
½ cup white vinegar
1 California orange
½ cup dry sherry
    Watercress
    Candied sweet potatoes
    Pineapple slices, halved

1 Tie legs of duckling together with string. Sprinkle 1 teaspoon salt into small roasting pan (this prevents duckling from sticking to pan). Place duckling, breast-side up, on salt.

2 Roast in hot oven (400°) 1 hour and 15 minutes; pour off fat from roasting pan; place chopped vegetables and bay leaves around duckling; mix with drippings. Roast 15 minutes longer. Transfer duckling to a heated platter; keep warm.

3 Turn vegetables and drippings into a medium-size saucepan. Skim off fat. Sprinkle flour over vegetables and stir in over medium heat. Add QUICK BROWN SAUCE and Madeira; cover. Simmer, stirring often, 10 minutes. Strain sauce.

4 Combine currant jelly, ½ cup of the sugar and vinegar in a medium-size saucepan. Cook over medium heat, stirring often, until mixture is thickened and syrupy (caramelized), about 10 minutes. Add to QUICK BROWN SAUCE mixture; cover. Simmer, stirring often, 30 minutes.

5 Cut one thin slice from orange for garnish, as pictured, if you wish. Peel the thin bright orange zest from orange with a vegetable parer. Cut zest into strips, ⅛-inch wide and 1½ inches long. Simmer strips in water to cover for 3 minutes; drain. Combine with remaining ½ cup of sugar and sherry in a small saucepan. Cook until orange strips are transparent and syrup is slightly thickened, 10 to 15 minutes. Stir into QUICK BROWN SAUCE mixture. (This is the Bigarade Sauce.) Cut orange into slices; reserve.

6 To serve duckling, arrange on platter with watercress, candied sweet potatoes and pineapple; spoon some of the sauce over duckling, cut reserved orange slices into quarters to garnish duckling; serve remaining sauce in a gravy boat.

Quick Brown Sauce

This sauce recipe can be used as a quick gravy substitute in other poultry dishes

Makes 2 cups.

3 tablespoons butter or margarine
¼ cup all-purpose flour
1 can condensed beef broth
⅔ cup water

1 Melt butter or margarine in small saucepan; stir in flour. Cook, stirring constantly, over low heat, until mixture turns golden brown. Remove from heat.

2 Stir in broth and water slowly. Continue cooking and stirring until sauce thickens and bubbles 1 minute; lower heat; simmer 5 minutes.

Springtime Party Platter

Dinner tonight can be festive, yet quick with Cornish Hens and delicate spring vegetables

Roast at 375° for 50 minutes.
Makes 2 servings.

2 frozen Cornish Hens, thawed (about 1½ pounds each)
3 tablespoons softened butter or margarine
2 teaspoons seasoned salt

¼ teaspoon pepper
¼ teaspoon leaf marjoram, crumbled
¼ cup dry white wine or chicken broth
1½ pounds fresh asparagus, trimmed and cooked
  OR: 1 package (10 ounces) frozen asparagus spears, cooked
2 small yellow squash, tipped and cut into sticks, cooked
2 tablespoons butter or margarine, melted
2 tablespoons chopped parsley

1 Rub hens with a mixture of softened butter or margarine, seasoned salt, pepper and marjoram.

2 Place in a 10x16-inch plastic cooking bag and seal, following label directions. Place in a shallow roasting pan.

3 Roast in a moderate oven (375°) 50 minutes, or until skin is golden; open plastic cooking bag carefully; place hens on a heated serving platter and surround with asparagus and yellow squash. Spoon melted butter or margarine and chopped parsley over vegetables.

4 Pour juices in cooking bag into a small saucepan; bring to boiling. Combine 2 tablespoons cold water with 1 tablespoon all-purpose flour in a cup; stir into boiling liquid; cook, stirring constantly, until sauce thickens and bubbles 3 minutes.

Golden-Crisp Cornish Hens

Little birds in coats of seasoned crumbs bake invitingly brown with no turning, no watching

Bake at 350° for 1 hour and 15 minutes.
Makes 6 servings

6 frozen Cornish Hens (about 1 pound each), thawed
  Salt
½ cup buttermilk
2 packages seasoned coating mix for chicken
1 package (1 pound) spinach noodles
½ teaspoon onion salt
2 tablespoons butter or margarine

1 Remove giblets from Cornish hens and chill to simmer for gravy another day. Rinse hens inside and out; pat dry. Sprinkle cavities lightly with salt.

2 Brush hens, one at a time, with buttermilk, then shake in coating mix. Place, breast side up and not touching, in a jelly-roll pan.

(continued)

3 Bake in moderate oven (350°) 1 hour and 15 minutes, or until tender and golden.
4 While hens bake, cook noodles in a kettle, following label directions; drain; return to kettle. Add onion salt and butter or margarine; toss lightly to mix.
5 Spoon noodles onto a large deep serving platter; arrange Cornish hens on top. Garnish with sprigs of water cress, if you wish.

ROASTING CHART

	Ready To Cook Weight	Oven Temp	Guide To Roasting Time
Domestic Duckling	3-5 lbs.	375°	1½-2¼ hrs.
Domestic Goose	7-9 lbs. 9-11 lbs. 11-13 lbs.	350° 350° 350°	2½-3 hrs. 3-3½ hrs. 3½-4 hrs.
Guinea Hen	1½-2 lbs. 2-2½ lbs.	375° 375°	¾-1 hr. 1-1½ hrs.
Cornish Game Hen	1-1½ lbs.	375°	1½ hrs.

Cornish Hen Platter

Brown these little birds, then bake in an herb-wine sauce and serve with pilaf

Bake at 350° for 1 hour.
Makes 8 servings

8 frozen Cornish Hens (about 1 pound each), thawed
¼ cup unsifted all-purpose flour
5 tablespoons butter or margarine
1 small onion, chopped (¼ cup)
1 can (13¾ ounces) chicken broth
1½ cups dry white wine
2 tablespoons chopped parsley
1 bay leaf
½ teaspoon leaf basil, crumbled
½ teaspoon leaf thyme, crumbled
½ teaspoon salt
¼ teaspoon pepper
2 tablespoons cornstarch
¼ cup cold water
Mushroom Pilaf (recipe follows)
1 can (about 1 pound, 14 ounces) peeled whole apricots, drained

1 can (1 pound, 14 ounces) sliced pineapple, drained
Sugared Grapes (recipe follows)

1 Rinse Cornish hens inside and out; pat dry. Sprinkle insides with salt and pepper; coat outsides lightly with flour. Brown, several at a time, in butter or margarine in a large frying pan; place in a large roasting pan.
2 Sauté onion until soft in drippings in same frying pan; stir in chicken broth, wine, parsley, bay leaf, basil, thyme, ½ teaspoon salt, and ¼ teaspoon pepper; pour into roasting pan; cover.
3 Bake in moderate oven (350°) 1 hour, or until hens are tender; lift out with a wide spatula and keep warm while making gravy.
4 Smooth cornstarch and water to a paste in a cup; stir into liquid in roasting pan. Cook, stirring constantly, until gravy thickens and boils 3 minutes; remove bay leaf.
5 When ready to serve, spoon *Mushroom Pilaf* onto a large serving platter; arrange Cornish hens in a circle on top. Place an apricot on each pineapple slice and arrange around edge of platter; tuck *Sugared Grapes* around pineapple. Garnish pilaf with a bouquet of celery tops, if you wish.
SUGARED GRAPES—Wash small clusters of seedless green grapes; dry well. Beat 1 egg white with ½ teaspoon water in a small bowl. Dip grapes into egg mixture, then roll in granulated sugar on waxed paper to coat well. Let stand on paper toweling to dry.

Mushroom Pilaf

Toasting the rice first gives it a wonderfully gourmet-like flavor

Makes 8 servings.

½ pound fresh mushrooms
OR: 2 cans (3 or 4 ounces each) chopped mushrooms
6 tablespoons olive oil or vegetable oil
2 cups uncooked regular rice
½ cup toasted slivered almonds (from a 5-ounce can)
2 tablespoons chopped parsley
1 teaspoon salt
3 envelopes instant chicken broth
OR: 3 chicken bouillon cubes
5 cups water

1 Wash fresh mushrooms; trim; chop. Sauté lightly in 2 tablespoons of the olive oil or vegetable oil in a large frying pan; remove with a slotted spoon and set aside. (If using canned mushrooms, set aside for Step 3.)

2 Stir rice and remaining 4 tablespoons olive oil or vegetable oil into same pan; heat slowly, stirring constantly, until rice is toasty-golden.

3 Stir in mushrooms (or canned mushrooms and liquid), almonds, parsley, salt, chicken broth or bouillon cubes, and water. Heat to boiling, crushing bouillon cubes, if used, with a spoon; cover.

4 Simmer 25 minutes, or until rice is tender and liquid is absorbed. Fluff up with a fork before serving.

Cornish Hens Indienne

Add to the subtle flavor of Cornish Hens with delicate herbs or spices

Roast at 375° for 1 hour and 20 minutes.
Makes 6 servings

6 *frozen Cornish Hens (about 1 pound each), thawed*
1½ *teaspoons salt*
¼ *teaspoon pepper*
¼ *teaspoon leaf thyme, crumbled*
½ *cup (1 stick) butter or margarine, melted*
4 *slices bacon, diced*
1 *medium-size onion, chopped (½ cup)*
1 *tablespoon flour*
1 *tablespoon sugar*
2 *teaspoons curry powder*
2 *teaspoons instant chicken bouillon*
1 *cup apricot nectar*
1 *tablespoon lemon juice*
Parsley Rice (recipe follows)
Buttered carrots

1 Remove giblets from body cavities of hens and save to simmer for soup. Rinse hens inside and out; pat dry with paper toweling.

2 Mix 1 teaspoon salt with pepper and thyme in a cup; sprinkle ¼ teaspoonful inside each hen; tie legs together. Place hens, breast side up, in a jelly-roll pan. Brush with part of the melted butter or margarine.

3 Roast in moderate oven (375°), brushing once or twice with remaining melted butter or margarine and drippings in pan, 1 hour. Cut away strings with scissors; spoon all drippings from pan.

(continued)

Small in size but strong in flavor, **Cornish Hens Indienne** is sure to delight any poultry lover.

4 While hens roast, sauté bacon until amost crisp in a medium-size saucepan; remove with a slotted spoon and drain on paper toweling. Stir onion into drippings; sauté until soft.

5 Blend in flour, sugar, curry powder, chicken bouillon, and ½ teaspoon salt; cook, stirring constantly, until bubbly. Stir in apricot nectar and lemon juice. Heat, stirring constantly, to boiling; simmer 5 minutes, or until mixture thickens slightly; spoon about half over hens.

6 Roast 10 minutes; spoon remaining curry mixture over top to make a thick coating. Continue roasting 10 minutes, or until hens are tender and richly glazed.

7 Spread *Parsley Rice* on a large deep serving platter; arrange hens on top. Spoon carrots at each end.

PARSLEY RICE—Combine 1 cup uncooked regular rice, 2 tablespoons butter or margarine, 2 teaspoons instant chicken bouillon, and 2¼ cups boiling water in a 6-cup baking dish; cover. Bake along with hens in moderate oven (375°) 1 hour, or until rice is tender and liquid is absorbed. Fluff rice with a fork; stir in ¼ cup chopped parsley. Makes 6 servings.

ALL ABOUT CORNISH HENS

This is a specially bred, very small chicken weighing 1½ pounds or less; it is available frozen in supermarkets across the country.

How Much To Buy: Allow 1 game hen per person.

East-West Broiled Cornish Hens

The flavor trick is, when broiling these little birds, to baste frequently with the marinade which keeps them especially moist

Makes 6 servings

3 frozen Cornish Hens (about 1 pound each), thawed
½ cup soy sauce
1½ cups water
2 green onions, trimmed and chopped
¼ teaspoon crushed red pepper
1 small head romaine, shredded (about 4 cups)
2 tablespoons dry sherry
Chinese noodles

1 Cut hens in half with poultry shears or kitchen scissors. Place in a large shallow broiling pan, without rack.

2 Combine soy sauce, ½ cup of the water, green onions and red pepper; pour over hens. Marinate 1 hour.

3 Broil hens, 4 inches from heat, turning often and basting with marinade, 40 minutes, or until hens are a rich brown.

4 Line a heated serving platter with shredded romaine. Arrange hens on romaine; keep warm.

5 Stir remaining 1 cup water and sherry into broiling pan.

6 Cook, stirring and scraping cooked-on bits from sides of pan, until liquid comes to boiling. Spoon over hens. Serve with Chinese noodles.

Roast Goose with Pumpernickel Dressing

In Germany, Christmas wouldn't be Christmas without roast goose: this one is stuffed with a rich pumpernickel dressing

1 frozen young goose, thawed (about 10 pounds)
2½ teaspoons salt
¾ teaspoon pepper
1 package (12 ounces) pitted, dried prunes
1 package (8 ounces) dried apricots
½ cup dry white wine
1 large onion, chopped (1 cup)
2 tablespoons butter or margarine
4 cups pumpernickel bread crumbs (8 slices)
2 medium-size apples, pared, cored and chopped

1 Thaw goose for 2 or 3 days in refrigerator. Remove giblets; also remove any large pieces of fat from inside goose. Sprinkle it inside and out with ½ teaspoon of the salt and ¼ teaspoon of pepper.

2 Dice prunes and apricots and place in a bowl.

3 Heat wine in a small saucepan; pour over fruits. Let stand 30 minutes to allow fruits to plump and absorb the wine.

4 Sauté onion in a small skillet in butter or margarine until soft.

5 Combine bread crumbs, chopped apples, onion, 2 teaspoons of the salt and ½ teaspoon of the pepper with the fruits and wine.

6 Stuff the goose lightly; fasten the opening with wooden picks or skewers; lace with string; tie legs together and fasten to tailpiece.

7 Place goose, breast-side up, on rack in a large roasting pan. Prick skin all over with a 2-tine fork so fat will cook out.

8 Roast goose in slow oven (325°) for 3 hours and 30 minutes, or until thick portion of drumstick is tender when pierced with fork. Makes 8 servings, plus enough for a bonus meal.

ALL ABOUT GOOSE

These birds are less frequently seen in supermarkets than chickens, turkeys or ducklings, but quick-frozen ones are beginning to appear in big city areas with some regularity. And, of course, they can be ordered. They are tender and rich and weigh anywhere from 5 to 15 pounds. Those weighing 9 to 12 pounds are best for stuffing and roasting.

How Much To Buy: Allow ¾ to 1 pound ready-to-cook goose per person.

Roast Goose with Fruit Stuffing

The traditional way to roast this festival bird

Roast at 325° for 3½ hours.
Makes 6 servings

1 frozen young goose (about 9 pounds)
1 package (11 ounces) mixed dried fruits
1 cup orange juice
10 slices white bread, toasted and diced
½ teaspoon ground ginger
½ teaspoon ground cinnamon
½ teaspoon ground nutmeg
¼ teaspoon ground cloves
Apricot brandy
Giblet Gravy (recipe follows)

1 Thaw goose 2 or 3 days in refrigerator. Remove giblets; also remove any large pieces of fat from inside goose. Rinse with cold water; drain.
2 Dice fruit; combine with orange juice in small bowl; let stand about 30 minutes.
3 Combine bread and spices in large bowl; pour fruit mixture over; toss until evenly moistened (mixture will seem somewhat dry).
4 Stuff about 1 cup fruit dressing in neck cavity; fold skin over and hold in place with wing tip or skewers.
5 Stuff remaining dressing into body cavity. Close vent with skewers or sew with needle and thread.

6 Place goose on rack in shallow pan; prick with two-tined fork in fatty areas around legs and wings. Do not cover; do not add water.
7 Roast in slow oven (325°) 1 hour; remove accumulated fat from pan. Drain fat twice more, roasting goose 3 hours in all. Brush goose with apricot brandy; roast 30 minutes longer, brushing with apricot brandy every 10 minutes. Remove to heated platter. To serve, carve breast into thin slices and separate drumsticks and thighs at joints. Garnish platter with chicory and red grapes, if you wish.

GIBLET GRAVY: Cook neck, gizzard, and heart in salted water in small saucepan (with celery tops, if you wish) 2 hours, or until tender; add liver; cook 15 minutes longer. Drain, adding water if needed to make 2 cups. Dice meat, discarding bone and gristle. Measure ¼ cup of drippings from roasting pan into medium-size saucepan; stir in ¼ cup of sifted all-purpose flour until blended. Stir in 2 cups broth; cook and stir until mixture thickens and boils 1 minute. Stir in diced meat and 1 tablespoon chopped parsley. Add salt and pepper to taste.

ROASTING CHART FOR BIRDS GAME

When you are presented with a game bird, pluck, draw, clean, and cool the bird as soon as possible. And take out the oil sac below the tail.

To help rid the bird of some of the gaminess, rub salt on the inside cavities. Then, after spooning in stuffing, fasten the bird by pulling back the neck skin and attaching it to the back with a small skewer. Tie legs to the tail and twist the wing tips under the back.

In a shallow roasting pan, place the bird, breast side up, on a rack. And brush the bird with cooking oil or melted butter. (Do not do this for wild duck.) Roast in uncovered pan according to the chart below. To prevent excess browning, place foil loosely over the top of the bird.

Bird	Cooking Weight	Oven Temp.	Roasting Time
Wild Duck	1½-2 lbs.	400°	1-1½ hrs.
Wild Goose	2-4 lbs. 4-6 lbs.	400°	1½-2 hrs. 2-3 hrs.

When you want to provoke discussion serve **California Chicken,** which is as varied as the state it is named for.

Poultry In The Crockery Pot

One of the most exciting up-dates of an old cooking method is here to stay. And it is a boon to the working homemaker. The old Dutch Oven has been given a new face with the introduction of the crockery pot. On these pages are favorite and new recipes that you put in the crockery pot in the morning—the cooked meal is ready when you return at night.

California Chicken

Crescents of avocado and tomato wedges add color as well as flavor to this chicken dish

Cook on 190° to 200° for 8 hours,
or on 290° to 300° for 4 hours.
Makes 6 servings.

3 whole chicken breasts, split (about 12 ounces each)
½ teaspoon salt
¼ teaspoon lemon-pepper
1 medium-size onion, chopped (½ cup)
1 teaspoon celery salt
¼ teaspoon leaf basil, crumbled
¼ teaspoon leaf marjoram, crumbled
½ cup dry sherry
1 tablespoon lemon juice
2 medium-size tomatoes
1 medium-size firm ripe avocado
  Pitted ripe olives
½ cup shredded Cheddar cheese

1 Arrange chicken breasts in an electric slow cooker and season with salt and lemon-pepper.
2 Combine onion, celery salt, basil, marjoram, sherry and lemon juice in a small bowl; pour over chicken. Cover slow cooker.
3 Cook on low (190° to 200°) 8 hours, or on high (290° to 300°) 4 hours.
4 Core tomatoes and cut into wedges. Halve, pit and peel avocado and cut into crescents; arrange around chicken breasts with olives; spoon juices in slow cooker over tomatoes; cover.
5 Cook 10 minutes; sprinkle cheese over chicken breasts; cook 5 minutes longer, or until cheese melts. Serve with a tossed salad and a chilled California white wine.

Dindonneau au Vin

Dindonneau is French for a young turkey: in this recipe it is simmered in wine and herbs

Cook on 190° to 200° for 9 hours,
then on 290° to 300° for 3 hours.
Makes 8 servings.

½ pound thickly sliced bacon
1 frozen turkey, thawed and cut up (about 6 pounds)
⅓ cup all-purpose flour
2 teaspoons salt
½ teaspoon freshly ground pepper
1 pound small white onions, peeled
2 cloves garlic, minced
3 cups dry red wine
2 sprigs parsley
2 sprigs celery leaves
1 bay leaf, broken
1½ teaspoons leaf thyme
½ pound mushrooms, quartered
3 tablespoons butter or margarine
16 baby carrots (from a 1-pound bag)
½ cup chicken broth
1 pound green beans, tipped
1 package (1 pound) noodles, cooked and drained

1 Cut bacon into 1-inch pieces; place in a small saucepan; cover with water. Bring to boiling; lower heat and simmer 10 minutes. Dry bacon on paper towels. Fry bacon until crisp, in an electric slow cooker with a browning unit or a large kettle. Remove bacon.
2 Shake turkey pieces with flour, salt and pepper in a plastic bag to coat well. Brown turkey, a few pieces at a time, in kettle; remove and reserve.
3 Brown onions in pan drippings until golden; stir in garlic and cook 2 minutes; stir in red wine and bring to boiling, scraping browned bits from bottom of kettle.
4 Place turkey and bacon in slow cooker; tie a bouquet garni of parsley, celery leaves, bay leaf and thyme in cheesecloth; push down into liquid in slow cooker; cover.
5 Cook on low (190° to 200°) 9 hours. Then on high (290° to 300°) 3 hours. Remove bouquet garni.
6 Thirty minutes before serving, wipe

(continued)

mushrooms with a damp towel. Sauté in butter or margarine in a large skillet until soft; remove and keep warm. Add carrots to skillet and sauté 3 minutes; pour chicken broth over; cover skillet; simmer 10 minutes; push carrots to one side; add green beans; cover skillet; simmer 15 minutes longer, or until vegetables are crisply-tender.
7 Spread cooked noodles on the bottom of a heated large platter; spoon turkey pieces and onions from slow cooker over noodles; arrange mushrooms, carrots and green beans on platter.

Caribbean Roast Chicken

Aromatic bitters and lemon juice add the flavors of the French West Indies to economical whole chicken

Cook on 190° to 200° for 10 hours,
or on 290° to 300° for 6 hours.
Makes 6 servings.

1 roasting chicken (about 4 pounds)
  SAVORY STUFFING (recipe follows)
¼ cup (½ stick) butter or margarine, melted
½ cup water
2 tablespoons lemon juice
1 teaspoon aromatic bitters
  LEMON SWIRL CUPS (recipe follows)
  Fresh spinach leaves

1 Stuff chicken neck and body cavities lightly with SAVORY STUFFING. Skewer neck to body; push tail inside bird and secure body cavity closed; tie legs together and draw string up and under wings and knot.
2 Brown chicken on all sides in butter in large skillet or electric slow cooker with browning unit.
3 Place chicken in slow cooker; add water, lemon juice and bitters; cover.
4 Cook on low (190° to 200°) 10 hours, or on high (290° to 300°) 6 hours. Arrange on a heated serving platter with LEMON SWIRL CUPS and fresh spinach leaves.
  LEMON SWIRL CUPS—Makes 2 cups. Hold a lemon vertically and make a one-half-inch lengthwise cut through the center with a sharp paring knife; make the second cut at a 45° angle to the first cut, starting at the base of the first cut. Continue this zig-zag cutting around center

of lemon until cuts meet. Pull apart to make cups.
  COOK'S TIP: If lemon does not separate easily after going around the first time, repeat, this time making the same cuts, but pushing knife deeper into fruit.

Savory Stuffing

Makes 2½ cups.

½ cup chopped celery leaves
2 tablespoons chopped onion
¼ cup (½ stick) butter or margarine
½ cup water
2 cups prepared bread stuffing mix (½ of an 8-ounce package)

1 Sauté celery leaves and onion in butter or margarine in medium-size saucepan. Add water; bring mixture to boiling.
2 Stir in bread stuffing; toss with fork just until moistened.

Old Country Chicken in the Pot

This is the kind of soup mother brought you when you were sick in bed

Cook on 190° to 200° for 8 hours,
or on 290° to 300° for 4 hours.
Makes 6 servings.

1 broiler-fryer, cut-up (about 3 pounds)
1 pound small new potatoes, washed
4 large carrots, pared and diced
2 white turnips, pared and diced
2 stalks celery with leaves, chopped
1 leek, trimmed and sliced
  OR: 1 large onion, chopped (1 cup)
1 tablespoon salt
6 cups water
  Handful parsley
6 peppercorns
1 bay leaf

1 Layer chicken, potatoes, carrots, turnips, celery and leek or onion in an electric slow cooker, sprinkling salt between layers; add water.
2 Tie parsley, peppercorns and bay leaf in a piece of cheesecloth. Push under liquid; cover.
3 Cook on low (190° to 200°) 8 hours, or on high (290° to 300°) 4 hours, or until chicken is tender. Ladle into soup bowl.

Aruba Chicken Sancocho

Caribbean fruit is paired with chicken and pork in this lively dinner-in-a-dish

Cook on 190° to 200° for 8 hours,
or on 290° to 300° for 4 hours.
Makes 8 servings.

1 Spanish onion, sliced
2 tablespoons olive oil or vegetable oil
1 broiler-fryer, cut-up (about 3 pounds)
1 pound smoked pork butt, cut into 1-inch cubes
2 tablespoons sherry cooking wine
2 cups water
1 can (8 ounces) tomato sauce
¼ cup flaked coconut
1½ teaspoons salt
½ teaspoon crushed red pepper
4 whole cloves
1 bay leaf
¼ teaspoon leaf thyme
2 pounds sweet potatoes
2 bananas, peeled and sliced ¾-inch thick
¼ cup sliced green onion

1 Sauté onion until golden in oil in a heavy skillet or an electric slow cooker with a browning unit, about 5 minutes. Remove and reserve.
2 Brown chicken, half at a time, in same pan, adding more oil if needed. Place chicken and onion in slow cooker. Add smoked pork and wine.
3 Stir in water, tomato sauce, coconut, and salt. Tie pepper, cloves, bay leaf and thyme in cheesecloth; add to slow cooker; pare sweet potatoes and cut into ½-inch slices. Add to slow cooker, pushing them down into liquid.
4 Cook on low (190° to 200°) 8 hours, or on high (290° to 300°) 4 hours, or until meats and potatoes are tender. Taste and add more salt if needed. (Salt content in pork varies.)
5 Stir bananas and green onions into stew. Cover and simmer 5 to 10 minutes longer. Arrange stew in serving dish. Garnish with additional coconut and green onion, if you wish.
SUGGESTED VARIATION: You can use 2 cups cubed cooked ham or bologna or 2 cups thickly sliced frankfurters for smoked pork.

Coriander Chicken

Coriander is an herb that is used extensively in North African cooking for a spicy yet fresh flavor

Cook on 190° to 200° for 8 hours,
or on 290° to 300° for 4 hours.
Makes 6 servings.

3 whole chicken breasts, split (about 12 ounces each)
¼ cup (½ stick) butter or margarine, melted
1 small onion, grated
1 tablespoon ground coriander
1½ teaspoons salt
½ cup chicken broth
1 tablespoon lemon juice
1 container (8 ounces) plain yogurt
2 tablespoons all-purpose flour

1 Roll chicken breasts in a mixture of melted butter or margarine, grated onion, coriander and salt in a pie plate to coat well.
2 Place in a 2½-quart electric slow cooker; pour chicken broth and lemon juice over; cover.
3 Cook on low (190° to 200°) 8 hours, or on high (290° to 300°) 4 hours, or until chicken is tender. Stir yogurt and flour together until well-blended in a small bowl. Stir into chicken, just before serving. Serve with rice pilaf and top with sliced green onions, if you wish.

Pot-Roasted Chicken

Beef broth and thyme are the flavor secrets to this French-style chicken dish

Cook on 190° to 200° for 10 hours,
or on 290° to 300° for 5 hours.
Makes 6 servings.

1 stewing chicken (about 5 pounds)
3 tablespoons butter or margarine
2 teaspoons leaf thyme, crumbled
1 can (10½ ounces) condensed beef broth
3 tablespoons all-purpose flour
1 small can evaporated milk

1 Brown chicken on all sides in butter or margarine and thyme until golden in a large skillet or an electric slow cooker with a browning unit.
2 Combine browned chicken and beef broth in slow cooker; cover.

(continued)

3 Cook on low (190° to 200°) 10 hours, or on high (290° to 300°) 5 hours, or until chicken is tender when pierced with a two-tined fork. Remove chicken to a heated platter and keep warm.
4 Turn heat control to high (290° to 300°). Combine flour and evaporated milk in a cup; stir into liquid in slow cooker until well-blended. Cover; cook 15 minutes. Taste and season with salt and pepper, if you wish. Serve sauce separately in heated gravy boat.

Chili Chicken

Serve this chili in deep soup bowls, but add forks as well as spoons: a salad of shredded lettuce and toasted corn chips are the perfect accompaniment

Cook on 290° to 300° for 2 hours,
then on 190° to 200° for 6 hours.
Makes 4 servings.

1 broiler-fryer, cut-up (about 3 pounds)
¼ cup all-purpose flour
2½ teaspoons salt
¼ teaspoon pepper
¼ cup vegetable shortening
1 large onion, chopped (1 cup)
1 clove garlic, minced
1 green pepper, halved, seeded and chopped
1 can (1 pound) tomatoes
1 can (10¾ ounces) condensed chicken broth
1 cup chopped ripe olives
½ cup yellow cornmeal
¼ cup tomato paste
1 to 3 tablespoons chili powder
1 teaspoon sugar

1 Shake chicken pieces in a mixture of flour, 1½ teaspoons of the salt and pepper in a plastic bag to coat evenly.
2 Brown chicken pieces in shortening in a large skillet or an electric slow cooker with a browning unit; remove and reserve. Pour off all but 2 tablespoons of the pan drippings. Sauté onion, garlic and green pepper in drippings until soft.
3 Place chicken pieces and onion mixture in slow cooker. Combine tomatoes, chicken broth, olives, cornmeal, tomato paste, chili powder, remaining 1 teaspoon salt and sugar in a medium size bowl, pour over chicken; cover.
4 Cook on high (290° to 300°) for 2 hours. Stir at this point. Turn heat control to low (190° to 200°) and cook 6 hours longer, or until chicken is tender.

Mississippi Chicken Dinner

Lima beans and green beans bubble along in the slow cooker with ripe olives and slices of tomato—so good, yet easy to prepare

Cook on 190° to 200° for 8 hours,
or on 290° to 300° for 4 hours.
Makes 8 servings.

2 broiler-fryers, quartered (about 2½ pounds each)
¼ cup all-purpose flour
2 teaspoons salt
1 teaspoon leaf basil, crumbled
¼ cup vegetable oil
1 clove garlic, minced
2 cans (1 pound each) cooked dried lima beans
1 can (1 pound) cut green beans, drained
½ cup sliced pitted ripe olives
4 medium-size firm ripe tomatoes, sliced ½-inch thick
½ cup dry white wine or water

1 Shake chicken pieces with a mixture of flour, salt and basil in a plastic bag to coat evenly.
2 Brown slowly in vegetable oil in a large skillet; remove and reserve. Sauté garlic in pan drippings until soft.
3 Stir in lima beans, green beans and ripe olives until well-blended.
4 Layer half the tomato slices, all of bean mixture and chicken in an electric slow cooker; top with remaining tomato slices; pour wine or water over; cover.
5 Cook on low (190° to 200°) 8 hours, or on high (290° to 300°) 4 hours, or until chicken is tender.

Memphis Burgoo

Burgoo is another name for stew: this one is filled with chicken, ham hocks, limas and okra

Cook on 190° to 200° for 8 hours,
or on 290° to 300° for 4 hours.
Makes 8 servings.

1 broiler-fryer (about 3 pounds)
2 smoked ham hocks (about 1 pound each)

4 cups water
2 large potatoes, pared and diced
2 large carrots, pared and diced
1 large onion, chopped (1 cup)
1 package (10 ounces) frozen Fordhook lima
  beans
2 cups shredded cabbage
1 cup sliced celery
1 large green pepper, halved, seeded and
  chopped
1 tablespoon Worcestershire sauce
2 teaspoons salt
½ teaspoon cayenne pepper
1 package (10 ounces) frozen whole okra,
  thawed
  Chopped parsley

1 Place chicken and ham hocks in a 5-quart slow cooker; add water, potatoes, carrots, onion, lima beans, cabbage, celery, green pepper, Worcestershire sauce, salt and cayenne; cover.
2 Cook on low (190° to 200°) 8 hours, or on high (290° to 300°) 4 hours, or until chicken is tender. Remove chicken and ham hocks from slow cooker. Cool.
3 Turn heat control to high (290° to 300°). Stir in okra and parsley; cover and cook 15 minutes.
4 While okra cooks, remove skin from chicken and ham hocks; take meat from bones, discarding fat; dice meat; return to slow cooker; cover.
5 Cook 10 minutes; ladle into heated soup bowls. Serve with corn bread or crusty hard rolls, if you wish.

Cape Cod Chicken

Cranberry and spices are the special flavor secrets of this festive chicken dish

Cook on 190° to 200° for 8 hours,
or on 290° to 300° for 4 hours.
Makes 8 servings.

2 broiler-fryers, quartered (about 2½ pounds
  each)
2 teaspoons salt
¼ cup vegetable oil
1 large onion, chopped (1 cup)
1 tablespoon grated orange rind
½ cup orange juice
3 tablespoons lemon juice
1 can (1 pound) whole-berry cranberry sauce
1½ teaspoons ground cinnamon
1½ teaspoons ground ginger

1 Rub chickens with salt to coat well. Brown, a few quarters at a time, in oil in a large skillet or an electric slow cooker with a browning unit; remove.
2 Sauté onion in pan drippings until soft; stir in orange rind and juice, lemon juice, cranberry sauce, cinnamon and ginger; bring to boiling, stirring constantly.
3 Combine chicken quarters and sauce in slow cooker; cover.
4 Cook on low (190° to 200°) 8 hours, or on high (290° to 300°) 4 hours, or until chicken is tender. Serve with fluffy rice and buttered peas, if you wish.

Santa Clara Chicken

Springtime vegetables are especially flavorful when you simmer them with chicken in a slow cooker

Cook on 190° to 200° for 10 hours,
or on 290° to 300° for 5 hours.
Makes 8 servings.

2 broiler-fryers, cut up (about 3 pounds each)
12 small new potatoes, pared
1 Bermuda onion, sliced thin
4 cups shredded lettuce
1 teaspoon salt
¼ teaspoon pepper
1 teaspoon leaf rosemary, crumbled
3 envelopes instant chicken broth
3 cups hot water
3 cups frozen peas, cooked (from a 1½-
  pound bag)
4 medium-size yellow squash, tipped, sliced
  and cooked
⅓ cup cornstarch
¾ cup water

1 Combine chicken with potatoes, onion, lettuce, salt, pepper and rosemary in a 5-quart electric slow cooker.
2 Dissolve instant chicken broth in hot water in 4-cup measure; pour over chicken and vegetables; cover.
3 Cook on low (190° to 200°) 10 hours, or on high (290° to 300°) 5 hours. Remove chicken and vegetables with a slotted spoon to the center of a heated serving platter; arrange

(continued)

cooked peas and squash in piles; keep warm while making sauce.

4 Strain juices in slow cooker into a large saucepan; bring to boiling. Combine cornstarch and ¾ cup water in a cup; stir into hot liquid; cook, stirring constantly, until mixture thickens and bubbles 1 minute; spoon over platter.

Chicken Quebec

Serving chicken flavored with bacon is a cooking secret French Canadians brought from France centuries ago

Cook on 190° to 200° for 10 hours,
or on 290° to 300° for 5 hours.
Makes 6 servings.

1 stewing chicken, cut up (about 5 pounds)
6 slices bacon
1 medium-size onion, chopped (½ cup)
1 teaspoon salt
½ teaspoon freshly ground pepper
4 cups water
1 package (8 ounces) elbow macaroni, cooked
1 tablespoon parsley flakes, crumbled

1 Trim fat from chicken; melt fat in a large skillet or an electric slow cooker with a browning unit. Brown chicken, a few pieces at a time in fat; drain.

2 Fry bacon lightly in same pan; remove and set aside; pour off all fat.

3 Place chicken and bacon in slow cooker; add onion, salt, pepper and water; cover cooker.

4 Cook on low (190° to 200°) 10 hours, or on high (290° to 300° 5 hours, or until chicken is tender.

5 Turn heat control to high (290° to 300°); add macaroni and parsley flakes. Cook 10 minutes; taste and season with additional salt and pepper, if you wish.

Drumstlcks Diable

Sweet and spicy best describes this chicken treat

Cook on 190° to 200° for 8 hours,
or on 290° to 300° for 4 hours.
Makes 4 servings.

8 drumsticks (about 2 pounds)
¼ cup all-purpose flour

1½ teaspoons salt
Dash pepper
3 tablespoons butter or margarine
1 can (1 pound) tomatoes
2 tablespoons brown sugar
2 tablespoons cider vinegar
2 tablespoons Worcestershire sauce
1 teaspoon chili powder
1 teaspoon dry mustard
½ teaspoon celery seeds
1 clove garlic, minced
Few drops bottled red-pepper seasoning

1 Shake drumsticks in a plastic bag with flour, ½ teaspoon of the salt and pepper.

2 Brown in butter or margarine in a large skillet or an electric slow cooker with a browning unit; remove.

3 Stir tomatoes, brown sugar, vinegar, Worcestershire sauce, chili powder, dry mustard, celery seeds, garlic and red-pepper seasoning into pan drippings; bring to boil, add remaining 1 teaspoon salt.

4 Combine drumsticks and sauce in slow cooker; cover.

5 Cook on low (190° to 200°) 8 hours, or on high (290° to 300°) 4 hours, or until chicken is tender. Serve with spaghetti.

Brunswick Stew

Meaty pieces of chicken cook lazily with corn and limas in a peppy tomato sauce

Cook on 190° to 200° for 8 hours,
or on 290° to 300° for 4 hours.
Makes 8 servings.

2 broiler-fryers, cut-up (about 2½ pounds each)
½ cup all-purpose flour
1 envelope (about 1 ounce) herb salad dressing mix
¼ cup vegetable shortening
1 large onion, chopped (1 cup)
1 can (1 pound, 12 ounces) tomatoes
Few drops bottled red-pepper seasoning
4 ears corn, husked and with silks removed, cut into 1-inch pieces
OR: 1 package (10 ounces) frozen whole-kernel corn, cooked
1 package (10 ounces) frozen Fordhook lima beans, cooked
1 pound okra, washed and cooked (optional)

1 Shake chicken in mixture of flour and salad dressing mix in a plastic bag to coat well; reserve any remaining flour.
2 Brown chicken, a few pieces at a time, in vegetable shortening in a large skillet or an electric slow cooker with browning unit. Remove and reserve.
3 Sauté onion in same pan; blend in reserved seasoned flour; stir in tomatoes and red-pepper seasoning. Bring to boiling, stirring constantly.
4 Place chicken and sauce in slow cooker; cover.
5 Cook on low (190° to 200°) 8 hours, or on high (290° to 300°) 4 hours. Add corn, lima beans and okra; cook 15 minutes longer.

Au Porto Chicken

Chicken in wine with a Portuguese touch—white Port is the cooking liquid: if you prefer a less sweet flavor, choose to dry white wine, such as Chablis

Cook on 190° to 200° for 10 hours,
or on 290° to 300° for 6 hours.
Makes 4 servings.

 1 broiler-fryer (about 3 pounds)
1½ teaspoons salt
 ½ teaspoon pepper
 1 large onion, chopped (1 cup)
 1 clove garlic, minced
 2 large carrots, pared and chopped
 2 tablespoons olive oil or vegetable oil
 1 teaspoon leaf rosemary, crumbled
 1 cup white Port or dry white wine or chicken
   broth
 ½ pound fresh mushrooms, quartered
   OR: 1 can (6 ounces) whole mushrooms
 2 tablespoons all-purpose flour
 ¼ cup cold water

1 Season chicken with ½ teaspoon of the salt and ¼ teaspoon of the pepper. Skewer neck skin to back and tie legs.
2 Sauté onion, garlic and carrots until soft in oil in a large skillet or 3½-quart electric slow cooker with a browning unit. Stir in remaining 1 teaspoon salt, ¼ teaspoon pepper and rosemary. Spoon into the bottom of electric slow cooker.
3 Place chicken on top of vegetables; pour in wine or chicken broth; cover.
4 Cook on low (190° to 200°) 10 hours, or on high (290° to 300°) 6 hours, or until chicken is tender when pierced with a two-tined fork.

Remove chicken to a heated platter and keep warm.
5 Turn heat control to high (290° to 300°). Add mushrooms and cook 15 minutes. Combine flour with ¼ cup cold water in a cup; stir into cooker until well-blended. Cover; simmer 15 minutes. Stir in a few drops bottled gravy coloring, if you wish. Slice chicken and pass sauce in heated gravy boat. Serve with a bottle of chilled dry white wine and a crisp salad of tossed greens with marinated artichokes, if you wish.

Slow Cooker Coq au Vin

Use a really good red Burgundy to get a great flavor. Flaming the brandy also does something delicious to the dish

Cook on 190° to 200° for 8 hours,
or on 290° to 300° for 4 hours.
Makes 4 servings.

 2 chicken breasts, split (about 12 ounces
   each)
 4 chicken legs or thighs
 ⅓ cup butter or margarine
 ¼ cup Brandy (optional)
12 small white onions, peeled
 2 cloves garlic, crushed
 ½ pound mushrooms, halved
 1 cup red Burgundy or dry red wine
 1 cup chicken broth
 1 teaspoon salt
 ¼ teaspoon pepper
 1 tablespoon chopped parsley
   Dash ground cloves
 ¼ teaspoon leaf thyme, crumbled
 1 bay leaf
 2 tablespoons cornstarch
 ¼ cup cold water

1 Brown chicken pieces in butter or margarine in a large skillet; warm brandy in a small saucepan; pour over chicken and flame; place in slow cooker.
2 Sauté onions, garlic and mushrooms in pan drippings; remove to slow cooker with a slotted spoon.
3 Stir in Burgundy wine, chicken broth, salt, pepper, parsley, cloves, thyme and bay leaf and bring to boiling, stirring up all the cooked-on bits in the bottom of the skillet; pour over chicken and vegetables; cover.
4 Cook on low (190° to 200°) 8 hours, or on high (290° to 300°) 4 hours, or until chicken
(continued)

is tender when pierced with a two-tined fork. Remove chicken and vegetables to a heated platter and keep warm while making gravy. Discard bay leaf.

5 Turn heat control to high (290° to 300°). Combine cornstarch and cold water in a cup to make a smooth paste; stir into sauce in slow cooker until well-blended. Cover; simmer 15 minutes longer to thicken sauce. Spoon sauce over chicken and serve with a bottle of the same hearty Burgundy used in the cooking and chunks of crusty French bread for soaking up the sauce.

Kentucky Chicken

Even folks who think they don't like lima beans will be sending their plates back for seconds

Cook on 190° to 200° for 10 hours,
or on 290° to 300° for 5 hours.
Makes 8 servings.

1 stewing chicken, cut-up (about 5 pounds)
½ cup all-purpose flour
1 envelope (about 1 ounce) herb salad dressing mix
3 tablespoons peanut oil
1 large onion, chopped (1 cup)
1 can (1 pound) tomatoes
2 cups diced celery
1 can (about 1 pound) lima beans
1 can (12 or 16 ounces) whole-kernel corn
1 package (10 ounces) frozen whole okra, thawed
1 can (4 ounces) pimiento, drained and chopped
¼ cup chopped parsley

1 Shake chicken with flour and salad dressing mix in plastic bag to coat evenly. Brown chicken in oil in a large skillet or an electric slow cooker with a browning unit; remove and reserve.
2 Sauté onion until soft in pan drippings; stir in tomatoes, celery, lima beans and corn; cover. (If using a skillet, place chicken and vegetables in slow cooker; cover.)
3 Cook on low (190° to 200°) 10 hours, or on high (290° to 300°) 5 hours, or until chicken is tender when pierced with a two-tined fork. Stir in okra and pimiento; cover and cook 15 minutes. Sprinkle with parsley just before serving.

Gala Fruited Chicken

All the flavor of tropical islands come together to plump chicken parts with sauce

Cook on 190° to 200° for 8 hours,
or on 290° to 300° for 4 hours.
Makes 6 servings.

1 roasting chicken, cut-up (about 5 pounds)
2 teaspoons paprika
1½ teaspoons salt
¼ teaspoon pepper
Dash cayenne pepper
3 tablespoons vegetable oil
1 can (8 ounces) crushed pineapple in pineapple juice
½ cup golden raisins
1 cup orange juice
½ cup dry white wine
⅛ teaspoon ground cinnamon
⅛ teaspoon ground allspice
2 California oranges, sectioned
½ cup toasted slivered almonds

1 Rub chicken pieces with a mixture of paprika, salt, pepper and cayenne. Brown in oil on all sides in a large skillet or an electric slow cooker with a browning unit.
2 Combine chicken pieces with crushed pineapple, raisins, orange juice, wine, cinnamon and allspice in slow cooker; cover cooker.
3 Cook on low (190° to 200°) 8 hours, or on high (290° to 300°) 4 hours, or until chicken is tender.
4 Lay orange sections over chicken and sprinkle with almonds; cook 15 minutes longer, just to heat through. Serve with fluffy rice, if you wish.

Carolina Chicken Stew

In some parts of the south, rabbit, rather than stewing chicken would have gone into the pot, but, either way, the long slow cooking flavor is there

Cook on 190° to 200° for 10 hours,
or on 290° to 300° for 5 hours.
Makes 8 servings.

1 stewing chicken, cut up (about 5 pounds)
2 large onions, peeled and sliced
1 large green pepper, seeded and sliced
¼ cup chopped parsley
1 tablespoon salt

1 tablespoon Worcestershire sauce
   Few drops bottled red pepper seasoning
1 package (10 ounces) frozen whole-kernel corn, thawed
1 package (10 ounces) frozen speckled butter beans or lima beans, thawed
1 can (1 pound) tomatoes, broken up
2 tablespoons cornstarch
¼ cup cold water

1 Arrange half the chicken parts in the bottom of an electric slow cooker; sprinkle with onion and green pepper slices and parsley.
2 Layer remaining chicken parts in cooker; season with salt, Worcestershire sauce and red-pepper seasoning; top with thawed corn, beans and tomatoes; cover slow cooker.
3 Cook on low (190° to 200°) 10 hours, or on high (290° to 300°) 5 hours, or until chicken is tender when pierced with a two-tined fork.
4 Turn heat control to high (290° to 300°). Combine cornstarch with ¼ cup cold water in a cup; stir into liquid in slow cooker until well-blended; cover; simmer 15 minutes. Serve with hot cornbread or baking powder biscuits.
SUGGESTED VARIATIONS: A tablespoon of chopped fresh oregano or marjoram leaves or a teaspoon of dried oregano or marjoram can be added for a more aromatic flavor.

Catalan Chicken

Simmer and serve this rich Spanish dish in your ever-helpful slow cooker

Cook on 190° to 200° for 10 hours,
or on 290° to 300° for 5 hours.
Makes 4 servings.

1 roasting chicken, cut up (3½ to 4 pounds)
3 tablespoons olive oil
1 teaspoon salt
3 medium-size onions, sliced
1 can (4 ounces) pimiento, sliced
2 medium-size tomatoes, peeled and chopped
2 tablespoons tomato paste
¼ cup water
¼ cup dry sherry
½ teaspoon sugar

1 Brown chicken pieces in oil with salt in a large kettle or an electric slow cooker with a browning unit. Remove.
2 Add sliced onions to pan and cook until soft.
3 Add pimiento, tomatoes, tomato paste, water, sherry and sugar to pan and bring to boiling.

4 Combine chicken and sauce in slow cooker; cover.
5 Cook on low (190° to 200°) 10 hours, or on high (290° to 300°) 5 hours. Serve with rice and crusty French bread.

Rosemary Chicken

Serve this flavorful chicken on the patio for a summer supper

Cook on 190° to 200° for 8 hours,
or on 290° to 300° for 4 hours.
Makes 4 servings.

2 broiler-fryers, cut-up (2 pounds each)
1 large onion, cut into thick slices
⅔ cup catsup
⅓ cup vinegar
¼ cup (½ stick) butter or margarine
1 clove garlic, minced
1 teaspoon leaf rosemary, crushed
1 teaspoon salt
¼ teaspoon dry mustard

1 Place chicken, skin-side down, in an electric slow cooker; top with onion slices.
2 Mix catsup, vinegar, butter or margarine, garlic, rosemary, salt and dry mustard in a small saucepan; bring just to boiling; pour over chicken.
3 Cook on low (190° to 200°) 8 hours, or on high (290° to 300°) 4 hours, or until tender.

Soy Simmered Chicken

Chicken quarters absorb piquant flavors from the soy-sherry sauce which glazes the chicken as it simmers

Cook on 190° to 200° for 10 hours,
or on 290° to 300° for 5 hours.
Makes 4 servings.

1 broiler-fryer, cut-up (about 3 pounds)
¼ cup water
¼ cup soy sauce
¼ cup dry sherry
¼ cup corn syrup
2 teaspoons seasoned salt

1 Combine water, soy sauce, sherry, corn syrup and seasoned salt in an electric slow cooker.

(continued)

2 Arrange chicken, skin-side down, in a slow cooker. Brush generously with part of the sauce; cover cooker.
3 Cook on low (190° to 200°) 10 hours, or on high (290° to 300°) 5 hours.

Pimiento Chicken Stew

A hearty meal topped with peppy pimiento biscuits

Cook on 190° to 200° for 10 hours,
or on 290° to 300° for 5 hours.
Makes 8 servings.

1 *stewing chicken, cut-up (4 to 5 pounds)*
½ *cup all-purpose flour*
1 *envelope (about 1 ounce) herb salad-dressing mix*
1 *large onion, chopped (1 cup)*
1 *can (1 pound, 13 ounces) tomatoes*
2 *cups water*
2 *cups diced celery*
2 *cups frozen lima beans*
2 *cups frozen whole-kernel corn*
1 *can (4 ounces) pimiento*
¼ *cup chopped parsley*
  PIMIENTO BISCUITS *(recipe follows)*

1 Remove all fat from chicken. Melt fat in large heavy skillet or an electric slow cooker with a browning unit.
2 Shake chicken with flour and herb salad-dressing mix in a plastic bag to coat evenly; brown, a few pieces at a time, in fat in pan. Remove chicken and reserve.
3 Sauté onion until soft in same pan; stir in tomatoes and water; add celery, lima beans, corn and chicken to slow cooker; cover.
4 Cook on low (190° to 200°) 10 hours, or on high (290° to 300°) 5 hours, or until chicken is tender; let stand 5 to 10 minutes; skim excess fat.
5 Save 1 pimiento for PIMIENTO BISCUITS; dice remaining; stir into stew with parsley; serve with PIMIENTO BISCUITS.

Pimiento Biscuits

Bake at 400° for 10 minutes.
Makes 12 biscuits.

1¾ *cups biscuit mix*
 ½ *cup yellow cornmeal*
 2 *tablespoons melted butter or margarine*

1 *pimiento, chopped*
⅔ *cup water*

1 Mix biscuit mix, cornmeal, melted butter or margarine and pimiento with a fork in a medium-size bowl; stir in water just until no dry mix appears; spoon in 12 mounds onto ungreased cooky sheet.
2 Bake in hot oven (400°) 10 minutes, or until golden.

Poulet en Casserole

This chicken dish is a standard on the menus of many gourmet restaurants

Cook on 190° to 200° for 10 hours,
or on 290° to 300° for 6 hours.
Makes 4 servings.

 1 *broiler-fryer (about 3 pounds)*
 2 *tablespoons vegetable oil*
 2 *tablespoons butter or margarine*
 2 *cloves garlic, minced*
12 *whole white onions, peeled*
12 *small white potatoes, pared*
 4 *large carrots, pared and quartered*
 1 *cup dry white wine*
 2 *teaspoons salt*
 1 *teaspoon leaf rosemary, crumbled*
 ½ *teaspoon freshly ground pepper*
 1 *can (10¾ ounces) condensed chicken broth*

1 Wash and dry chicken; skewer neck skin to back; twist the wing tips flat against skewered neck skin; tie the legs to tail with kitchen string.
2 Heat oil and butter or margarine with the minced garlic in a large skillet or an electric slow cooker with a browning unit. Brown chicken in the hot fat; remove.
3 Sauté onions, potatoes and carrots in drippings; remove and reserve. Stir wine, salt, rosemary and pepper into pan and bring to boiling, scraping up all the cooked-on juices from bottom of pan; stir in chicken broth; place chicken in slow cooker; surround with browned vegetables and sauce; cover.
4 Cook on low (190° to 200°) 10 hours, or on high (290° to 300°) 6 hours, or until chicken is tender. Garnish with a bouquet of parsley and serve with a chilled dry white wine, such as a Chablis, and chunks of crusty French bread, if you wish.

Melbourne Chicken

This delectable chicken has a light curry-and-fruit-flavored sauce

Cook on 190° to 200° for 6 hours,
or on 290° to 300° for 3 hours.
Makes 8 servings.

4 whole chicken breasts (about 12 ounces each)
3 tablespoons all-purpose flour
1 tablespoon curry powder
2 teaspoons salt
¼ cup vegetable oil
1 tablespoon sugar
2 envelopes instant beef broth or 2 beef bouillon cubes
1 large onion, chopped (1 cup)
1 cup water
1 jar (about 5 ounces) baby-pack apricots
2 tablespoons lemon juice
2 teaspoons soy sauce

1 Pull skin from chicken breasts; halve each.
2 Shake with mixture of flour, curry powder and salt in a plastic bag to coat lightly and evenly.
3 Brown pieces in vegetable oil in a large skillet or an electric slow cooker with browning unit; remove and reserve.
4 Stir sugar, beef broth or bouillon cubes, onion, water, apricots, lemon juice and soy sauce into drippings in pan; heat to boiling, crushing bouillon cubes, if used, with a spoon. Pour over chicken in slow cooker; cover.
5 Cook on low (190° to 200°) 6 hours, or on high (290° to 300°) 3 hours. Serve over hot fluffy rice or noodles.

Halved Chicken Italiano

Chicken halves are simmered in an herbed tomato sauce and served over hot spaghetti

Cook on 190° to 200° for 10 hours,
or on 290° to 300° for 5 hours.
Makes 4 servings.

2 broiler-fryers, split (2½ pounds each)
1 tablespoon vegetable oil
1 green pepper, halved and seeded
1 large onion, chopped (1 cup)
1 clove garlic, crushed
1 can (8 ounces) tomato sauce
½ cup dry red wine
1 teaspoon mixed Italian herbs, crumbled

Dash ground cloves
1 package (½ pound) spaghetti
2 tablespoons butter or margarine
1 tomato, cut into wedges
3 tablespoons chopped parsley
½ teaspoon salt

1 Brown chicken in oil in a large skillet or an electric slow cooker with a browning unit. Remove halves as they brown; keep warm.
2 Chop ½ the green pepper; cut other half into strips; reserve strips. Sauté the chopped pepper, onion and garlic until soft in same pan. Stir in tomato sauce, wine, Italian herbs and cloves. Bring to boiling. Combine chicken in slow cooker with sauce; cover.
3 Cook on low (190° to 200°) 10 hours, or on high (290° to 300°) 5 hours.
4 Thirty minutes before serving, cook spaghetti, following label directions; drain. Place on large heated platter.
5 While spaghetti is cooking, sauté pepper strips in butter or margarine in small skillet; add tomato wedges, parsley and salt; cook 2 minutes longer, or just until tomato is soft. Arrange chicken halves on hot spaghetti. Spoon sauce over. Garnish with sautéed pepper-tomato mixture on top of the sauce.

Chicken Orléans

This superb dish is named for the Ile d'Orléans near Quebec City, which is noted for its apple orchards

Cook on 190° to 200° for 8 hours,
or on 290° to 300° for 4 hours.
Makes 4 servings.

1 broiler-fryer (about 3 pounds)
Apple brandy or cognac
1 teaspoon salt
¼ teaspoon freshly ground pepper
2 cups diced white bread (4 slices)
½ cup chopped celery
½ cup chopped apple
¼ cup raisins
3 tablespoons butter or margarine, melted
1 tablespoon chopped parsley
½ teaspoon leaf thyme, crumbled
3 slices thickly-sliced bacon
6 medium-size apples
1 cup light cream

(continued)

1 Rub chicken inside and out with brandy or cognac, then with salt and pepper.
2 Combine bread cubes, celery, chopped apple, raisins, butter or margarine, parsley and thyme in a bowl.
3 Stuff chicken with dressing, packing lightly. Skewer neck skin to back; twist the wing tips flat against skewered neck skin; tie legs to tail with kitchen string.
4 Place bacon in a saucepan; cover with water. Bring to boiling; lower heat and simmer 10 minutes. Dry on paper towels.
5 Fry bacon lightly in an electric slow cooker with a browning unit or a large kettle. Remove bacon and reserve. Brown chicken on all sides in bacon drippings; remove and keep warm.
6 Quarter, core and thickly slice apples; brown lightly in pan drippings. Place chicken on top of apple slices in slow cooker; lay bacon slices over chicken; cover cooker.
7 Cook on low (190° to 200°) 8 hours, or on high (290° to 300°) 4 hours, or until chicken is tender. Pour cream and 2 tablespoons apple brandy or Cognac over, just before serving.

3 Brown chicken, a few pieces at a time, in bacon drippings; reserve.
4 Sauté onion and garlic until soft in same pan; stir in reserved flour mixture. Drain liquid from mushrooms. Stir liquid, tomatoes, parsley and the red pepper seasoning into pan; bring to boiling, stirring constantly.
5 Spoon over chicken in slow cooker; cover.
6 Cook on low (190° to 200°) 10 hours, or on high (290° to 300°) 5 hours. Uncover; sprinkle with saved bacon pieces and mushrooms. Sprinkle GOLDEN CROUTONS over top; garnish with more chopped parsley.

GOLDEN CROUTONS—Makes 1 cup. Trim crusts from 2 slices of white bread; cut into ½-inch cubes. Spread in single layer in shallow baking pan. Toast in moderate oven (350°) 10 minutes, or until golden.
Hostess Tip: This dish is even more delicious when made ahead, removed from slow cooker, cooled and refrigerated until one hour before serving time. Heat in moderate oven (350°) 1 hour, or until bubbly; top with croutons and parsley.

Chicken Marengo

This dish is said to have been developed by Napoleon's chef after the Battle of Marengo from ingredients he had on hand

Cook on 190° to 200° for 10 hours,
or on 290° to 300° for 5 hours.
Makes 8 servings.

6 slices bacon, cut in 1-inch pieces
2 broiler-fryers, cut-up (about 3 pounds each)
½ cup all-purpose flour
2 teaspoons salt
¼ teaspoon pepper
1 large onion, chopped (1 cup)
1 clove garlic, minced
1 can (3 or 4 ounces) whole mushrooms
2 cans (1 pound each) tomatoes
¼ cup chopped parsley
  Few drops bottled red-pepper seasoning
  GOLDEN CROUTONS (recipe follows)

1 Fry bacon until almost crisp in large skillet or electric slow cooker with a browning unit. Lift out with slotted spoon; drain on paper towels and reserve. Leave drippings in pan.
2 Shake chicken in mixture of flour, salt and pepper in plastic bag to coat well; reserve remaining flour.

Mexicali Chicken

Chicken and peppers are steeped in a tangy tomato sauce

Cook on 190° to 200° for 10 hours,
or on 290° to 300° for 5 hours.
Makes 8 servings.

2 broiler-fryers, cut up (about 3 pounds each)
2 tablespoons butter or margarine
2 tablespoons olive oil or vegetable oil
1 large onion, chopped (1 cup)
1 large green pepper, halved, seeded, and chopped
1 large sweet red pepper, halved, seeded and chopped
1 tablespoon chili powder
¼ cup all-purpose flour
1 can (about 2 pounds) Italian tomatoes
1 tablespoon salt
¼ teaspoon pepper

1 Brown chicken, part at a time, in butter or margarine and oil in a large skillet or an electric slow cooker with a browning unit; remove and reserve.
2 Stir onion and green and red peppers into drippings in pan; sauté until soft. Stir in chili powder; cook 1 minute longer.

3 Sprinkle flour over top, then blend in; stir in tomatoes, salt and pepper. Cook, stirring constantly, until sauce thickens and bubbles 3 minutes.
4 Layer browned chicken, topping each piece with part of the sauce, into slow cooker; cover.
5 Cook on low (190° to 200°) 10 hours, or on high (290° to 300°) 5 hours. Garnish with rings of red and green pepper, if you wish.

Chicken Cacciatore

This is the Italian version of Chicken Hunter-style, with pieces of chicken and green pepper in wine-tomato sauce

Cook on 190° to 200° for 8 hours, or on 290° to 300° for 4 hours. Makes 6 servings.

2 broiler-fryers, cut-up (about 2½ pounds each)
⅓ cup all-purpose flour
2 teaspoons salt
¼ teaspoon freshly ground pepper
1 large onion, chopped (1 cup)
2 cloves garlic, minced
¼ cup olive oil or vegetable oil
2 large green peppers, halved, seeded and cut into chunks
½ cup dry white wine
1 can (1 pound, 1 ounce) Italian tomatoes
Hot linguini or thin spaghetti

1 Shake chicken pieces in a mixture of flour, salt and pepper in a plastic bag.
2 Sauté onion and garlic in 2 tablespoons of the oil until soft in a large skillet or an electric slow cooker with a browning unit. Remove with slotted spoon and reserve.
3 Brown chicken, a few pieces at a time, adding remaining oil as needed; remove and reserve. Sauté peppers in drippings until soft; stir in wine; bring to boiling, stirring constantly. Return onion and garlic to pan; stir in tomatoes.
4 Place chicken in slow cooker; spoon sauce over chicken; cover.
5 Cook on low (190° to 200°) 8 hours, or on high (290° to 300°) 4 hours. Sprinkle with chopped parsley, if you wish. Serve with linguini or thin spaghetti.
SUGGESTED VARIATION: *Chicken Chasseur:* This is the French version of Chicken Hunter-style. It is named in honor of the famous Chasseur cavalry regiments who hunted for their food.

Follow the recipe for *Chicken Cacciatore,* except use ½ cup chopped shallots or green onions instead of the yellow onions. Substitute 1 cup brown gravy for the wine and ½ pound sliced fresh mushrooms or 1 can (6 ounces) sliced mushrooms for the green peppers. Sprinkle with chopped parsley and serve with boiled potatoes.

Brown Chicken Fricassee

Chicken browned with onions and topped off with cornmeal dumplings should please all

Cook on 190° to 200° for 10 hours, or on 290° to 300° for 5 hours. Makes 6 servings.

1 stewing chicken, cut-up (about 5 pounds)
¼ cup all-purpose flour
2 teaspoons salt
1 teaspoon poultry seasoning
¼ teaspoon pepper
3 tablespoons vegetable oil
2 medium-size onions sliced and separated into rings
1 bay leaf
4 cups water
CORNMEAL DUMPLINGS (recipe follows)

1 Shake chicken pieces, a few at a time, in mixture of flour, salt, poultry seasoning and pepper in a plastic bag to coat well.
2 Brown chicken slowly in oil in a large skillet or an electric slow cooker with a browning unit; remove and reserve. Add onion rings, sauté until soft, about 3 minutes.
3 Return chicken to slow cooker; add bay leaf and water; cover.
4 Cook on low (190° to 200°) 10 hours, or on high (290° to 300°) 5 hours.
5 Prepare CORNMEAL DUMPLINGS: Turn heat control to high (290° to 300°); drop dough into 12 small mounds on top of fricassee; cover cooker.
6 Cook 30 minutes. (No peeking, or the dumplings won't puff properly.) Serve chicken and dumplings right from cooker.
CORNMEAL DUMPLINGS—Makes 12 dumplings. Sift 1½ cups sifted all-purpose flour, ¼ cup yellow cornmeal, 1 tablespoon baking powder and 1 teaspoon salt into a medium-size bowl. Cut in 2 tablespoons shortening with a pastry blender until mixture is crumbly. Stir in 1 cup milk just until flour mixture is moistened. (Dough will be soft.)

Garden Chicken

Fresh asparagus, new potatoes and celery combine with chicken quarters in this meal-in-one dish

Cook on 190° to 200° for 10 hours,
or on 290° to 300° for 5 hours.
Makes 4 servings.

    1 broiler-fryer, quartered (about 3 pounds)
1½ teaspoons salt
    1 teaspoon leaf tarragon, crumbled
    2 tablespoons butter or margarine
    1 pound small new potatoes, pared
    2 tablespoons chopped chives
    2 tablespoons chopped parsley
 ½ cup dry white wine
    2 cups sliced celery, cooked and drained
    1 pound asparagus (break off ends of stems where they snap easily), cooked and drained
    1 tablespoon lemon juice

1 Sprinkle chicken on both sides with ½ teaspoon of the salt and ½ teaspoon tarragon. Heat butter or margarine in large skillet or an electric slow cooker with a browning unit; add chicken, skin-side down, and brown slowly; turn, and brown other side; remove and reserve.
2 Add potatoes to the butter in skillet; cook slowly over low heat for about 5 minutes and add to slow cooker with chicken. Sprinkle chicken and potatoes with chives, parsley and drippings from pan and wine; cover slow cooker.
3 Cook on low (190° to 200°) 10 hours, or on high (290° to 300°) 5 hours.
4 Ten minutes before serving, add celery pieces and asparagus. Sprinkle vegetables with remaining 1 teaspoon salt and ½ teaspoon tarragon; spoon juices in slow cooker over asparagus and celery. Drizzle with lemon juice.
5 Cover and cook 5 minutes longer, or until chicken and vegetables are tender; baste occasionally with the juices in slow cooker.

Roman Forum Chicken

Flavorful red pimiento, black olives, mushrooms and white wine blend in this tempting Roman chicken-spaghetti dish

Cook on 190° to 200° for 8 hours,
or on 290° to 300° for 4 hours.
Makes 8 servings.

    2 broiler-fryers, cut-up (2½ to 3 pounds each)
 ½ cup all-purpose flour
    2 teaspoons salt
 ¼ teaspoon pepper
 ¼ cup olive oil
    1 clove garlic, crushed
 ¼ cup chopped parsley
 ½ teaspoon poultry seasoning
      Dash bottled red-pepper seasoning
    1 cup dry white wine
 ¾ cup pitted ripe olives, sliced
    1 can (6 ounces) sliced mushrooms
    1 can (4 ounces) pimiento, drained and cut into large pieces
      PARSLEY-BUTTERED SPAGHETTI (recipe follows)

1 Roll chicken pieces in flour, salt and pepper on wax paper; then brown in hot oil in a large heavy skillet or an electric slow cooker with a browning unit.
2 Mix garlic, parsley, poultry seasoning, red-pepper seasoning and wine; pour over browned chicken; simmer a few minutes.
3 Scatter olives, mushrooms, and pimiento pieces over chicken and wine mixture in slow cooker; cover.
4 Cook on low (190° to 200°) 8 hours, or on high (290° to 300°) 4 hours.
5 Serve hot with PARSLEY-BUTTERED SPAGHETTI and pass a bowl of grated Parmesan cheese.

PARSLEY-BUTTERED SPAGHETTI—Cook 1 package (1 pound) thin spaghetti according to package directions. Drain and toss with ¼ cup melted butter or margarine (½ stick) and with 1 cup chopped parsley.

INDEX